University
Meets Microfinance

Partner IOO68994

In Collaboration with:

- Université Libre de Bruxelles / Belgium
- ESCEM / France
- ESC Dijon / France
- Sciences Po / France
- Freie Universität Berlin / Germany
- Leibniz Universität Hannover / Germany
- Eberhard Karls Universität Tübingen / Germany
- Rjiksuniversiteit Groningen / The Netherlands

- Frankfurt School of Finance and Management / Germany
- Università Cattolica del Sacro Cuore Milano / Italy
- Università degli Studi di Bergamo / Italy
- Università degli Studi di Roma "La Sapienza" / Italy
- Universidade Católica Portuguesa / Portugal
- Universidade Nova de Lisboa / Portugal
- European Microfinance Platform (e-MFP)

We thank the following professors and practitioners for having participated in the Selection Committee: Ashta Arvind (ESC Dijon), Diego Dagradi and Maria Cristina Negro (Fondazione Giordano Dell'Amore), Marie-Anne de Villepin (BNP Paribas), Oliver Gloede (Leibniz University Hannover), Philippe Guichandut (Grameen Crédit Agricole), Hansjorg Leo Kessler (FIDES), Katja Kirchstein (Freie Universität Berlin), Thilo Klein (University of Cambridge), Roland Knorren (ACCION), Julien Lacombe (Microcred), Christina May (Universität Köln), Klaas Molenaar and Julie-Marthe Lehmann (INHolland) Margherita Mori (Università degli Studi dell' Aquila), Roberto Moro Visconti (Università Cattolica del Sacro Cuore), Ahmad Nawaz (Universität Göttingen), Lucia Poletti (Università degli Studi di Parma), Marie Pons, Vincenzo Provenzano (Università degli Studi di Palermo), Jessica Schicks (Université Libre de Bruxelles), Baptiste Venet (Université Paris Dauphine), Laura Viganò and Davide Castellani (Università degli studi di Bergamo) as well as Eliane Augareils, Delphine Bazalgette, Pauline Bensoussan, Maud Chalamet, Frances Fraser, Gabrielle Harris, Miquel Jordana and Vanessa Quintero (PlaNet Finance).

With the Financial Support of:

escem   SOGETI   **BOMBARDIER** The Global Leader in Rail Technology   *ERNST & YOUNG* Quality In Everything We Do   Capgemini CONSULTING TECHNOLOGY OUTSOURCING   sanofi aventis

With Kind Support of:

Allianz SE, BNP Paribas, Frankfurt School of Finance and Management and Dexia Kommunalbank Deutschland AG supported UMM activities (workshop, scholarship)

Collaboration with European Microfinance Platform

In 2010 the European Microfinance Platform (e-MFP) has set up an e-MFP Action Group "University Meets Microfinance" for practitioners to work with European universities and further enhance students' research and microfinance professionalization.

EUROPEAN
MICROFINANCE
PLATFORM

UNIVERSITY MEETS MICROFINANCE

edited by PlaNet Finance Deutschland e.V.

ISSN 2190-2291

The "University Meets Microfinance" Programme (UMM) presents its seventh "UMM Award":
Each year the UMM Awards honour outstanding theses on microfinance and give recognition to the work of young researchers. The UMM Award winners are selected by a committee of professors and microfinance practitioners, to recognize these presenting innovative research topics and approaches.
Microfinance has gained scale and recognition over the last decade. Today, Microfinance Institutions reach approximately 190 million low-income people, who were previously excluded from formal banking systems, with financial services which include credit, savings, insurance and money transfer. This rapid expansion has also come with increasing challenges.
Research on microfinance provides new insights into these challenges and can foster innovation in the sector.
As of today UMM events gathered 1886 students, professors and practitioners from 10 European countries. The Programme is co-financed by the European Union and was initiated by PlaNet Finance and Freie Universität Berlin with the aim of strengthening the cooperation between European universities and microfinance practitioners. In addition to promoting research publications, UMM offers microfinance seminars in partnership with European universities, mentorship and field research scholarship for Bachelor, Master and PhD students and organizes regular workshops with UMM participants.

More information can be found at
www.universitymeetsmicrofinance.eu and www.planetfinance.org

Volumes

4   *Oliver Rogall*
    Microfinance and Vulnerability to Poverty
    The Evidence from Rural Households in Cambodia
    ISBN 978-3-8382-0237-2

5   *Maria Cristina De Lorenzo*
    Microfinance Investment Funds: An analysis of profitability
    ISBN 978-3-8382-0251-8

6   *Sascha Huijsman*
    The Impact of the Current Economic and Financial Crisis on Microfinance
    ISBN 978-3-8382-0235-8

7   *Funmilayo A. Akinosi, Daniel Nordlund, Alejandro Turbay*
    Sustainable Microfinance
    Redefining the Socio-Economic Mission in Microfinance
    ISBN 978-3-8382-0334-8

Funmilayo A. Akinosi, Daniel Nordlund, Alejandro Turbay

SUSTAINABLE MICROFINANCE

Redefining the Socio-Economic Mission in Microfinance

ibidem-Verlag
Stuttgart

Bibliografische Information der Deutschen Nationalbibliothek
Die Deutsche Nationalbibliothek verzeichnet diese Publikation in der
Deutschen Nationalbibliografie; detaillierte bibliografische Daten sind im
Internet über http://dnb.d-nb.de abrufbar.

Bibliographic information published by the Deutsche Nationalbibliothek
Die Deutsche Nationalbibliothek lists this publication in the Deutsche Nationalbibliografie;
detailed bibliographic data are available in the Internet at http://dnb.d-nb.de.

∞

Gedruckt auf alterungsbeständigem, säurefreien Papier
Printed on acid-free paper

ISSN: 2190-2291

ISBN-13: 978-3-8382-0334-8

© *ibidem*-Verlag
Stuttgart 2012

Printed in Germany

Preface

Increasing scientific evidence tells us that the impacts our society is having on the biosphere are currently unsustainable. In contexts when the sustainability issues and how to tackle them are brought up, it is often argued that economically wealthier countries should do more to drastically reduce their negative contributions to the root causes of the problem. It is also easy to recognize that for such countries with a higher GDP per capita there is an enormous potential to dematerialize their material flows while keeping the same quality of life: what is often argued is that we can 'decouple' our quality of life from our dependence on the negative trends that will ultimately destroy the very capacity of the biosphere to sustain us. Doing more with less, reducing and ultimately eliminating our dependance on some destructive trends. Climate change mitigation lends itself as a very poignant example in this case. Since the cumulative contribution to the accumulation of CO_2 in the atmosphere has been largely due to emissions from high GDP countries in the last decades, such nations should be equally responsible to make drastic reductions in their emissions in the coming years. This all sounds reasonable and is easy to agree upon.

What is harder to bring into the conversation is the role of growing economies in this effort towards a sustainable society. When the needs to increase the GDP (as a proxy, though very inaccurate, for quality of life) take priority on the agenda of a fast developing country it may happen that the negative and unsustainable impacts are seen as a necessary trade-off for a wealthy economy. In the worst case, they are seen as a luxury that poor countries cannot afford yet. Thankfully, many positive trends in the recent years are calling for a complete reframing of this issue.

Environmental sustainability and social sustainability are seen as strongly connected to one another: our capacity to face environmental issues such as a successful management of commonly owned resources is highly connected to social trust and how well a society is doing. On the other hand, a pre-condition for fostering a society free of conflicts is the assumption that the satisfaction of basic human needs is met. On a local level, often this satisfaction is entirely dependant upon environmental sustainability: it is hard to bring about peace and social justice without access to clean water, a sustainable food production, or the preservation of a forest.

This link between ecological and social sustainability is becoming all the more apparent, independently of the status of economic growth of a country.

In October 2009, Bill McKibben launched the first global day of action to advocate for drastic reductions of CO_2 emissions. People participating from all over the world showed their sense of urgency and their readiness to change course. What was really new was the dismantling of the old myth that only richer countries can "afford" actions such as environmental preservation or climate change mitigation. What global sustainability movements are showing, the world over, is that developing nations are not considering anymore the "either economic progress or a safe environment" dichotomy, but are recognizing that one cannot exist without the other.

In the growing field of microfinance there haven't been many studies of how loans be leveraged from the lens of a scientific approach to strategic sustainable development. The work that is introduced here is a commendable exploration of this link. I have had the pleasure to be thesis advisor for the initial work on which this book is based upon and I witnessed a solid link between the need for a unifying understanding of the sustainability issue and an application to the microfinance world. This link will make the case very relevant to the reader who is interested in contributing positively to poverty alleviation while using a robust understanding of the sustainability challenge and how to address it as upstream as possible.

Marco Valente
Karlskrona, December 2011
Project assistant at the Masters in Strategic Leadership Towards Sustainability
(Blekinge Institute of Technology)

Acknowledgements

We thank our advisors, Mr Marco Valente and Dr Edith Callaghan, for their support through the thesis period. We also thank Tamara Connell, the Programme Director, and the staff of the Master's in Strategic Leadership towards Sustainability programme at the Blekinge Institute of Technology.

We are also grateful to the professionals within the microfinance sector, who, despite their busy schedules, contributed to our research by answering our questions and giving us feedback.

- Mr Robert Annibale: Global Director, CitiMicrofinance
- Ms R.V. Aparna: Head Process, Asirvad Microfinance
- Ms Deborah Drake: Vice President, Investment Policy and Analysis, Accion International
- Ms Bunmi Lawson: Managing Director/CEO, Accion Microfinance Bank Limited
- Ms Karen Losse: Senior Advisor, Financial Systems Development, Deutsche Gesellschaft für Internationale Zusammenarbeit (GIZ) GmbH
- Mr Soumalya Mandal: Programme Manager, Microfinance Vivekananda Sevakendra-O-Sishu Uddyan-VSSU
- Ms Carol Mulwa: Country Manager Oikocredit Kenya
- Mr Akintunde Oyebode: Head SME Banking, Stanbic IBTC Bank Plc., Nigeria
- Mr Dean Pallen: Principal at Dean Pallen International
- Mr N.K. Ramakrishna: Founder and CEO of RangDe
- Ms Anna Ritz: Former employee at Tujijenge Microfinance (TMF)
- Mr D Sattaiah: Chief Operating Officer of BASIX
- Haroon Sharif, Head (Economic Growth Group), Department for International Development (DFID), Islamabad, Pakistan
- Mr Lokesh Singh: Co-founder and Managing Partner at Sanchetna India
- Mr Anton van Elteren: Senior Environmental & Social Specialist, FMO
- Ms Jessica Villanueva: MIF Program Coordinator at Inter-American Development Bank

8 Acknowledgements

We thank our peer advisors and classmates for their views and the shared learning experiences that made writing this thesis a truly enjoyable experience.

Funmilayo Akinosi, Daniel Nordlund, Alejandro Turbay

Acknowledgements

We thank our advisors, Mr Marco Valente and Dr Edith Callaghan, for their support through the thesis period. We also thank Tamara Connell, the Programme Director, and the staff of the Master's in Strategic Leadership towards Sustainability programme at the Blekinge Institute of Technology.

We are also grateful to the professionals within the microfinance sector, who, despite their busy schedules, contributed to our research by answering our questions and giving us feedback.

- Mr Robert Annibale: Global Director, CitiMicrofinance
- Ms R.V. Aparna: Head Process, Asirvad Microfinance
- Ms Deborah Drake: Vice President, Investment Policy and Analysis, Accion International
- Ms Bunmi Lawson: Managing Director/CEO, Accion Microfinance Bank Limited
- Ms Karen Losse: Senior Advisor, Financial Systems Development, Deutsche Gesellschaft für Internationale Zusammenarbeit (GIZ) GmbH
- Mr Soumalya Mandal: Programme Manager, Microfinance Vivekananda Sevakendra-O-Sishu Uddyan-VSSU
- Ms Carol Mulwa: Country Manager Oikocredit Kenya
- Mr Akintunde Oyebode: Head SME Banking, Stanbic IBTC Bank Plc., Nigeria
- Mr Dean Pallen: Principal at Dean Pallen International
- Mr N.K. Ramakrishna: Founder and CEO of RangDe
- Ms Anna Ritz: Former employee at Tujijenge Microfinance (TMF)
- Mr D Sattaiah: Chief Operating Officer of BASIX
- Haroon Sharif, Head (Economic Growth Group), Department for International Development (DFID), Islamabad, Pakistan
- Mr Lokesh Singh: Co-founder and Managing Partner at Sanchetna India
- Mr Anton van Elteren: Senior Environmental & Social Specialist, FMO
- Ms Jessica Villanueva: MIF Program Coordinator at Inter-American Development Bank

8 Acknowledgements

We thank our peer advisors and classmates for their views and the shared learning experiences that made writing this thesis a truly enjoyable experience.

Funmilayo Akinosi, Daniel Nordlund, Alejandro Turbay

Executive Summary

Rationale for Research

Thomas Edison predicted the end of poverty by 2011 (Cosmopolitan 1911). This prolific American inventor, whose development of the electric light bulb influenced life as we know it, assuredly stated that "poverty was for a world that used only its hands" (ibid.). He insisted that, as men used their brains in an industrialised process, poverty would decrease. Sadly, Edison was wrong. Recent estimates place the rate of poverty in the developing world at one in five people (Chen and Ravallion 2007), amounting to 1.4 billion people living in extreme poverty (IBRD / World Bank 2008a). Our industrialised world is still faced with "poverty", defined by a "denial of choices" and lack of capacity to effectively participate in society (United Nations 1998).

Policymakers have unsuccessfully tried to reduce poverty using mechanisms such as foreign aid. Over time, microfinance – the provision of access to small loans by poor people – has emerged as a viable method for this purpose. The rationale is that financial access, when combined with complementary business training, can stimulate entrepreneurship and economic well-being, as opposed to aid or relief, which makes the recipient dependent.

The "fight against poverty" through the use of microfinance has been largely based on socio-economic considerations. This is largely because the immediate basic needs of subsistence usually seem more pressing than ecological considerations. Two major views on the poverty-environmental link have emerged. The first is supported by the Brundtland Commission and other international agencies and holds that poverty is one of the primary causes of environmental degradation (Brundtland Report 1987). The second view sees the poor's contributions to environmental degradation as minimal in comparison to more affluent economies.

Despite the differences in opinion, it is increasingly clear that the poor suffer more from ecological mismanagement, as they are more "dependent on agriculture and other climate-sensitive natural resources and well-being" that are linked to ecological considerations (IPCC 2007; Skoufias, Rabassa, Olivieri, and Brahmbhatt 2011, 1). Micro-enterprises, which are also recipients of microcredit, have also been identified as being in one of the most vulnerable sectors to environmental hazards (Summit Conference on Sustainable Development, Santa Cruz, Bolivia, 1996, 1996a; IBRD / World Bank 2008b). Further, environmental factors such as natural hazards and harvest failure due to drought or flooding are characteristic of the high levels of insecurity and risk associated with lending to the poor (Matin, Hulme, and Rutherford 2002, 275; Pallen 2011). Sustainable development extends beyond adapting to such ecological challenges. Unlike adaptation, which merely involves making changes to accommodate growing problems, with mitigation measures, planners find the roots or "go upstream" to find the origins of the problems and address them.

Our thesis explored the idea that microfinance can best foster sustainable development when it is "integrated in a view of community development that links the social, economic and environmental dimensions" (Vargas 2000). We considered microfinance institutions (MFIs) that are fundamentally socio-economically focussed rather than those with primarily "financial inclusion" missions. We suggest that aligning MFIs with a sustainable development perspective can mitigate poverty in an ecologically and socially sustainable manner (Lal and Israel 2006).

Research Framework

In defining an MFI operating in a sustainable manner, we used the Framework for Strategic Sustainable Development (FSSD), a systematic and strategic approach to sustainable development, built around a concrete scientific-based framework for sustainability (Holmberg and Robèrt 2002, 294).

The FSSD comprises five distinct but interrelated levels: systems, success, strategic, actions, and tools. The systems level includes an appreciation of the interrelations between the society and the ecosphere. The success level refers to achieving the goals for the system. "Success" is defined within the Sustainability Principles, which are presented in Chapter 1.6.1. The strategic level describes the prioritisation process for the actions that have been produced on the fourth level of the FSSD. The tools implement and manage the chosen actions and measure success. Tools may also be strategic and help to understand whether or how the actions chosen fit with the strategic guidelines and methods, as well as make direct measures in the system to monitor damage or improvement based on actions taken in society.

The Sustainability Principles are a set of four ecological and social conditions created through an interdisciplinary, peer-reviewed procedure that identified the conditions for a sustainable society. We also used the concept of *backcasting* – a methodology where a planner decides on the process from the desired state of success towards the current circumstances. In relation to this thesis, our desired state of success was a socio-economic mission-driven microfinance institution, which carried out its operations in a sustainable manner, as defined by the Sustainability Principles.

Our research questions were:

1. How would socio-economic mission-driven microfinance institutions (MFIs) operate using a full sustainability perspective?
2. What are the major conditions under which socio-economic mission-driven MFIs presently operate?
3. What are some strategic moves that these MFIs can take in this regard?

Methods

Our research was structured in three iterative phases: creation of a model, gathering of data and data analysis, and model testing. Utilising the backcasting approach to planning, we created a vision of the model socio-economic mission-driven microfinance institution that has taken a full sustainability perspective. We then interviewed a number of professionals whom we identified as experts in their fields. Questions asked during the data-gathering phase were primarily aimed at formulating the current reality of socio-economic mission-driven microfinance institutions in relation to their existing structure and work on ecological sustainability. The third phase involved sending the model to experts, who we had interviewed in the first phase, for testing and receiving feedback on possible improvements.

Results

The results were presented using the first three levels of the FSSD (systems, success, strategic). Actions and tools were not included as they are usually for individual MFIs. In the first section, we provided information on a microfinance institution that carries out its socio-economic mission in an ecologically beneficial manner, while the second was an overview of the current reality.

Discussions

Chapter 4 primarily provides an analysis of the results stated in the previous chapter. We observed that a full sustainability perspective would help meet the challenges and maximise the opportunities discovered while gathering data for the current reality. These challenges and opportunities were grouped into three categories: managing credit risk, enhancing reputation, and minimising competition; improvement of the bottom line; and organisational learning.

We also suggested a prioritisation process for MFIs based on the three prioritisation questions suggested by the FSSD within the context of microfinance. This was done in order to be able to propose strategic actions when starting to move towards sustainability.

Conclusion

Socio-economic mission-driven microfinance institutions traditionally focus on the "double bottom line", i.e., measurement of performance by profit and social impact. Ecological considerations are increasingly coming to the forefront, although they are largely deemed as external to what are seen as the more immediate social needs.

We suggest that a full sustainability perspective that includes environmental considerations would help MFIs address pressing challenges as well as present them with significant opportunities. We also show that this perspective can aid these MFIs in strategically meeting their goals. The FSSD provides a beneficial framework that a socio-economic mission-driven MFI can use to plan for success. We also provided suggestions for some strategic moves, which are highlighted below:

Establish the Foundation. In order to act strategically, it is important that the organisation appreciates the sustainability challenge and the rationale for moving towards sustainability. We suggest that executive management engage stakeholders and agree on defining the vision, core values, and mission within the Sustainability Principles.

Leverage on Loan Process. The loan process offers a high leverage point for MFIs to maximise the socio-economic and ecological benefits. There are existing strategic guidelines available such as Netherlands Development Finance Company's (FMO) sustainability guidance e-toolkit and Canadian International Developmental Association's (CIDA) Environmental Sourcebook for MFIs. These can be used towards screening less beneficial projects and enhance potentially sustainable ones.

Build Staff Capacity. Consistent training and capacity-building can help boost an organisation's development. There are many advantages to this such as increased efficiency to reach the goals and higher retention of staff.

Offer Complementary Products and Services. Business and health training has been shown to reduce loan defaults. From the borrower's perspective, there are many benefits such as empowerment, capacity-building, and improved ecological conditions.

Connect with Impact Investors. Socio-economic mission-driven MFIs who are forward-thinking and work with environmental initiatives can seek out impact investors, development banks, and funds that support these initiatives at favourable loan conditions.

Emphasise External Communications. MFIs can differentiate themselves and improve their reputation and competitiveness by communicating the positive things they and their clients are doing in the socio-economic arena.

Glossary

Backcasting: A planning method where planners start by building a vision of success in the future, and then ask: "What do we need to do today to reach this vision?"

Biosphere: The earth's surface area, from the upper limits of the atmosphere to the lower layers of the soil, both on land and in the ocean. It is also referred to as the ecosphere.

Double Bottom Line: It is often used to describe investments that have a social component and refers to social returns as economic profits.

Ecological Economics: This is a transdisciplinary field of academic research that aims to address the interdependence and co-evolution of human economies and natural ecosystems over time and space.

Ecosystem Services: Humankind benefits from many resources and processes that are provided by nature and natural resources. These benefits are known as ecosystem services and include products such as clean drinking water and fertile soil.

Financial Inclusion: Delivery of financial services at affordable costs to sections of disadvantaged and low-income segments of society.

Framework for Strategic Sustainable Development (FSSD): A concrete scientific-based framework for sustainability planning and making decisions towards sustainable development.

Microfinance: The provision of financial services such as credit, savings, and insurance to low-income clients or solidarity lending groups, including consumers and the self-employed, who traditionally lack access to banking and related services.

Microfinance Institutions (MFIs): These are institutions that provide financial services such as credit, savings, and insurance to low-income clients who traditionally lack access to credit, banking, and related services.

Socio-economic: This is also referred to as "social economics" and refers to the use of economics in the study of society. In this thesis, MFIs that articulate social and economic missions are referred to as being "socio-economic" mission-driven.

Sustainability: This implies the potential for long-term maintenance of well-being, which has environmental, economic, and social dimensions.

Sustainability Challenge: This implies the systematic errors of societal design that are driving humans' unsustainable efforts in the socio-ecological system (interactions between the biosphere and human society). It also includes an appreciation of the serious obstacles to fixing those errors, and the opportunities for society if those obstacles are overcome.

Sustainable Development: This is the active transition from the current globally unsustainable society towards a sustainable society. Once the transition is complete, it refers to further social development within that society.

Sustainability Principles (SPs): The four basic principles for a sustainable society in the biosphere, underpinned by scientific laws and knowledge, comprise the four Sustainability Principles:

In a sustainable society, nature is not subject to systematically increasing:
1. concentrations of substances extracted from the Earth's crust;
2. concentrations of substances produced by society;
3. degradation by physical means; and, in that society...
4. people are not subject to conditions that systematically undermine their capacity to meet their needs.

Systems Thinking: It is the ability to understand and address the whole, while examining the interrelationship between the parts.

Triple Bottom Line: This is also referred to as "people, planet, profit" and "the three pillars". It captures an expanded spectrum of values and criteria for measuring organisational and societal success: economic, ecological, and social.

Table of Contents

List of Figures and Tables

1 Background

1.1 The Challenge: Poverty as a Barrier

> *"Poverty is a denial of choices and opportunities, a violation of human dignity. It means lack of basic capacity to participate effectively in society."* *(United Nations 1998).*

Recent estimates place the rate of poverty in the developing world at one in five people (Chen and Ravallion 2007), amounting to 1.4 billion people living in extreme poverty (IBRD / World Bank 2008a). There is rich and insightful research on defining "poverty" (Kirchgeorg and Winn 2006; Chen and Ravallion 2008; Chen, Ravallion, and Sangruala 2008; Alkire and Santos 2010). For the purpose of this thesis, we considered poverty in light of the UN's general depiction: a barrier and the lack of capacity to meet one's needs. This agrees with a significant amount of literature from Booth's "line of poverty" (Booth 1887) to other works focusing in this area (Atkinson 1987; Gillie 1996; Kawani 1993). We have placed emphasis on developing economies, where statistics show a high level of poverty.

"Needs" and the means by which they are satisfied have also been explained in other literature (Maslow 1943; Max-Neef, Elizalde and Hopenhayn 1991). A recurring thread in these is financial capital, which could help satisfy them. For example, physiological or subsistence needs could be satisfied by food or heat, often requiring some form of monetary exchange. It is therefore generally accepted that economic empowerment is a leverage to mitigate poverty, as it prompts a rise in average income levels (Vargas 2000, 11; Roemer and Gugerty 1997).

Empowering the poor or the alleviation of poverty could be done in different ways. Matin, Hulme, and Rutherford describe the "initial wave of faith" of state-mediated and subsidised credit used to reduce poverty and another wave of deregulated financial markets (Matin, Hulme, and Rutherford 2002, 274). In the post–World War II era, low-income countries had provided heavy subsidies to banks in order to develop their agricultural sectors (Armendáriz and Morduch 2010, 9; Kono and Takahashi 2009, 17). This was aimed at increasing land productivity, labour demand, and agricultural wages. While the intensions may have been good, these moves led to a repressed financial system in low-income countries and corruption as the cheap loans became politically administered and distributed to typically well-off farmers (Armendáriz and Morduch 2010, 9–10). Aid has also been shown to fail as a poverty reduction tool since it often goes to the governments in the first instance and rarely reaches the ultimate beneficiaries (Hillman 2002, 788).

Rather than aid or relief that usually makes the recipient dependent, financing by loans (and in some cases, with business training) is argued to be better poised to deal with poverty due to the entrepreneurial angle. In this way, the poor can begin income-generating business as an alternative to infrequent and inefficient handouts. The clichéd maxim – teach a person to fish rather than feed her – may be one way to describe this.

In theory, access to financial services by way of loans and deposit facilities would provide financial leverage, incite entrepreneurial projects, and translate to increased business, thereby prompting a better standard of living. In reality, lending to the poor is not as simple. Small credits required by the poor carry a higher cost of operations (Schreiner 2001; Olivares-Polanco 2005, 56). This comes from direct and indirect transaction costs, as the unit of transaction is generally miniscule (Matin, Hulme, and Rutherford 2002, 275). This is worsened by the insecurity and financial risks associated with providing credit and other banking facilities to the poor, who rarely have credit records or steady income that incentivise commercial lending. This is also emphasised by difficulties of contract enforcement due to weak judicial systems in some developing economies that make it more difficult to finance clients with little or no collateral or marketable assets. A sector has therefore emerged to provide the required financial services to fuel this empowerment and induce an increase in income levels.

1.2 Defining the Language

Contemporary literature often uses the terms "microcredit" and "microfinance" interchangeably. For instance, the Microcredit Summit Campaign describes microcredit as "the extension of small loans and other financial services such as savings accounts to the very poor" (The Microcredit Summit Campaign 2010).

However, microcredit is only one aspect of microfinance (Arora and Meenu 2010; Cornford 2002; Armendáriz and Morduch 2010, 15). Armendáriz and Morduch explain that "microcredit" was initially coined to refer to Grameen Bank-type institutions that gave loans to the poor and were explicitly focussed on poverty reduction and social change, while "microfinance" came with the recognition of the need for additional financial services as savings (Armendáriz and Morduch 2010, 15). They explain that the change in language has come with a change in orientation with microfinance providing an emphasis on the "less poor" (ibid.).

On the other hand, Cornford as well as Arora and Meenu differentiate between "microfinance" (the provision of a range of financial services including savings, loans, insurance, leasing) and "microcredit" (microloans to low-income micro-enterprises and households) (Arora and Meenu 2010, 45; Cornford 2002, 344). Cornford goes further to explain that the use of the term "microcredit" is associated with an inadequate appreciation of the value of savings services to the poor and that in most cases, the provision of savings services in "microcredit" schemes simply involve the collection of compulsory deposits that are designed to collateralise the loan (Cornford 2002, 344).

An analogous term is "microenterprise". There is no universal definition as it depends on the country's stage of development, policy objectives, and administration (World Bank 1978, 18). In this thesis, we loosely ascribed this to mean clients of MFIs.

All definitions agree that the introduction of the suffix "micro-" assumes a focus on the provision of access to small amounts of capital. The fine lines drawn may have little practical effect, as the credit and savings aspect of microfinance are the most developed (Arora and Meenu 2010, 45) with very minimal financial activity outside of these two.

In our thesis, we have used the term "microfinance institutions" (MFIs) in reference to institutions that provide microcredit. Some of these institutions also provide complementary services.

1.3 Microcredit: Trends

Microcredit has received increasing attention as an effective means of empowering the poor (United Nations General Assembly 2000). In 1995, the UN-sponsored World Summit for Social Development underscored the significance of improving access to microcredit (Resolution 52/194). By 1998, the UN General Assembly, with Resolution A/RES/53/197, designated 2005 as the International Year of Microcredit and attempted to link the eradication of poverty with the strengthening of microcredit institutions (United Nations General Assembly 1998). In 2006, the Nobel Committee awarded Dr Muhammad Yunus and Grameen Bank the Nobel Peace Prize for their efforts in creating socio-economic development through microcredit (Nobel Prize 2010). Yunus is a Bangladeshi economist who founded Grameen Bank in the 1970s. The UN also emphasised the significance of microfinance for private sector development and its role in creating wealth and enhancing financial self-sufficiency for low-income people (United Nations Capital Development Fund 2005, 3).

Microcredit has enabled borrowers to develop and diversify their businesses as well as reduce dependence on informal moneylenders and reduce poverty (Agricultural Finance Corporation Limited 2008; Arora and Meenu 2010, 49). It has also helped promote social and economic capital for women – a form of "solidarity" that builds a collective consciousness towards resistance of oppression (Rankin 2006, 86).

Microcredit has, however, faced a large amount of criticism. Primarily, it is condemned as creating barriers in place of those it purports to lift by institutionalising poverty as it locks borrowers into long-term loans with high interest rates. MFIs have also been accused of profiting from the poor. Even Muhammad Yunus expressed concerns about the misapplication of microfinance by investment funds, which he referred to as the "new loan sharks" (MacFarquhar 2010). Other researchers have argued that non-credit and more direct income-generating interventions are required for the poorer whom "poverty escape through credit" is too much risk and inappropriate (Hashemi 1997; Greeley 1997). Critics also point out that MFIs approach only the "wealthier poor", who can make repayments (Arora and Menu 2010, 49), and that microcredit is ineffective as a poverty reduction measure for the *ultra-poor,* who are already indebted (Haque and Yamao 2008). Still, literature on group dynamics suggest tensions in group lending such as abuse by group leaders, particularly the executive officers as the presidents and treasurers, as well as power inequalities between representatives and the rest of the members (Marr 2002; Mercado 1999).

In spite of these criticisms, the history of microfinance shows a substantial track record of accomplishments, and a significant body of empirical studies shows its impact as an effective antipoverty and development strategy (Wright 2000; Zaman 2000; Khandker 2001). More importantly, poverty is "a multidimensional problem, embedded in a complex and interconnected political, economic, cultural, and ecological system" (United Nations 2007). It may therefore be the case that the criticisms lie in the dismissal of the problem of persistent poverty that necessitated its application in the first place (Hilson and Ackah-Baidoo 2010, 2). Microfinance cannot be the sole solution for poverty reduction because poverty is itself multidimensional. However, it offers one way to help the poor "manage their financial needs and deal with shocks" (Sharif 2011).

Some researchers have argued that the challenges with microcredit lie with the design, rather than the concept itself (Kaushal and Kala 2005, 2; Wright 2000) and that success lies with the appropriate product design and targeting (Wright 2000; Nitin and Tang 2001) and additional efforts (Arora and Menu 2010, 49).

1.4 Microfinance: Socio-economic Considerations

By itself, lending to the poor is not a novel concept. The informal lending sector, which includes traditional moneylenders, pawnbrokers, relatives, trade-specific lenders, and deposit takers, had thrived as a source of financial capital as part of the local culture in a number of countries such as Nigeria (Ikeanyibe 2010, 124). Studies in 2006, for example, showed that local moneylenders provided approximately 80 per cent of the total amount borrowed in a district in India (Sriram and Parhi 2006). Another study showed that many of the medium and small enterprises were also using friends and relatives as the major source of finance (Ageba Amha 2006).

The informal sector has a number of advantages. It offers easy and relatively quick disbursement of credit that is useful for emergencies and consumption; there are minimal procedural formalities; as well as minimal collateral requirements. Further, lenders in this sector have information on borrowers, which mitigates risk and minimises default risk caused by an adverse selection of borrowers (Armendáriz and Morduch 2010, 9; Kono and Takahashi 2009, 16). The informal sector also provides effective means of enforcing contracts through social networks. However, informal lenders, especially "moneylenders", often have negative connotations of exploitation and very high interest rates. They also have limited resources (Armendáriz and Morduch 2010, 9).

Microfinance, as we know it, emerged as a niche market for semi-formal (and with increasing regulation, formal) banking services for small-scale credit to the poor. Unlike the typical banking model, Grameen Bank relied on the borrower's social ties within the community. Thus, instead of physical collateral, the bank would lend to voluntarily formed groups on a joint liability basis rather than to the individual. While the idea of rotating credit groups is as old as commerce itself (Rankin 2006, 85), its rise to mainstream prominence as a development strategy coincided with the proliferation of Grameen-type banks. Other institutions, usually registered as NGOs, also began providing these services. Over time, a large number of microfinance institutions have either converted to formal banks, such as PRODEM to BancoSol in Bolivia, or have become highly regulated, and can hardly be considered semi-formal (Matin, Hulme, and Rutherford 2002, 278).

1.5 Ecological Considerations

1.5.1 The Poverty Perspective

Conventional wisdom views poverty as one of the primary causes of environmental degradation. The Brundtland Report, "Our Common Future", which is regarded as an authoritative document on sustainable development, lists poverty as the first symptom and cause of environmental degradation (Brundtland Report 1987). According to the report, the pressure of poverty pollutes the environment, creating environmental stress cumulating from overcrowding of cities, deforestation, overharvesting of grasslands, and overuse of marginal land (Brundtland Report 1987). The report's sentiments were echoed by the World Bank's Environment Strategy, which affirmed that "population, poverty, and environmental degradation are inextricably linked" (World Bank 2001).

The Brundtland Commission's views have, however, been questioned and deemed a simplistic generalisation of conceptions of environmental degradation (Leach and Mearns, 1995) and in some cases, found incorrect (Broad 1994). Another researcher claims that the "hypothesis of a poverty-environment link" is based on "anecdotal evidence", as there has been little to establish the relative importance of the economic activities of the poor and non-poor in explaining environmental degradation (Ravnborg 2003, 1933–1934, 1944). In fact Ravnborg goes on to show how environmental degradation was predominantly due to the farming practices of the most prosperous farmers (Ravnborg 2003, 1944). On the arguments against a poverty-environmental link, history shows the rise of socio-economic conditions during the industrialisation age came with attendant pollution. More so, in 2008, the relatively affluent United States, for example, generated 19 per cent of the world's CO_2 emissions (International Energy Agency 2010). The rise of socio-economic conditions for affluent economies led to increased extraction and use of resources, causing a depletion of common ecosystem services they depend on. An example of this would be overfishing in northern Canada, causing the collapse of the Northern Cod fishery (Hamilton, Haedrich, and Duncan 2004, 195). This is an example of degradation of ecosystems "upstream" that could be dealt with through mitigation, whereas attending and adapting to pollution caused elsewhere is an example of adaptation.

However, it is clear that developing economies and their poor are often more "dependent on agriculture and other climate-sensitive natural resources and well-being" that are linked to ecological considerations (IPCC 2007; Skoufias, Rabassa, Olivieri, and Brahmbhatt 2011, 1). Specifically, micro-enterprises, which are recipients of microcredit, have been identified as one of the most vulnerable sectors to environmental hazards (Summit Conference on Sustainable Development, Santa Cruz, Bolivia, 1996, 1996a; The Independent Evaluation Group 2008). Environmental factors such as natural hazards and harvest failure due to drought or flooding have also been found to be characteristic of the high levels of insecurity and risk associated with lending to the poor (Matin, Hulme and Rutherford 2002, 275; Pallen 2011).

Consequently, whether or not ecological mismanagement predominantly results from poverty, it largely affects the poor's livelihood through its effects on health, access to water and natural resources, homes, and infrastructure (Skoufias, Rabassa, Olivieri, and Brahmbhatt 2011, 2). The Intergovernmental Panel on Climate Change (IPCC) report estimates that climate change-induced exposure to increased water stress in some African countries by 2020 would affect between 75 million and 250 million people (IPCC 2007, 444). However, Europe seems more adaptable to water management challenges with "well-documented" strategies (IPCC 2007, 559). It is therefore prudent that any poverty alleviation tool maximises its utility within frameworks that take the environment into consideration. There is also an important opportunity for MFIs to address upstream reductions of contributions to the sustainability challenge mentioned earlier. By addressing these problems upstream, MFIs would be strategic and preventive by mitigating their own and their clients' environmental impacts instead of merely adapting to the sustainability challenge that affects them both.

1.5.2 An Integrated Approach: Socio-economic Considerations within Ecological Beneficial Limits

Microfinance institutions are traditionally premised on the socio-economic angle: provision of access to financial services as a means of alleviating poverty. The familiar argument is that the typical client of an MFI is motivated by the need for immediate survival and short-term income rather than environmental protection. Ecological standards are also deemed as an additional burden on the poor, since more affluent economies contribute more to the increasing degradation and do not seem to face stringent ecological standards. Policymakers face this "difficult dilemma" in choosing between ignoring the environmental consequences of micro-enterprise activities so as to "promote short-term growth or craft cost-effective and practical mitigation strategies" (Wenner, Wright, and Lal 2004, 98). It does not help that money flows from the market economy do not usually reflect ecosystem considerations (Gowdy and Erickson 2005, 219). As Costanza et al. put it, "ecosystem services are not fully 'captured' in commercial markets or adequately quantified in terms comparable with economic services and manufactured capital (and) are often given too little weight in policy decisions" (Costanza et al. 1997, 253).

Yet, as explained in the previous subsection, the consequences of economic actions cannot be separated from the natural environment in which the actors operate (Lal and Israel 2006). Access to credit has environmental resource consequences through increased economic activity from capital investment and changes in borrowers' income, which, unhindered, may increase resource use and waste production (Anderson, Locker, and Nugent 2002, 96).

A significant amount of literature shows that full sustainability implies resilience and vitality of the economic, social, and environmental subsystems (Rademacher 2004; Kirchgeorg and Winn 2006, 172), rather than merely one subsystem. Aligning microfinance with a sustainable development perspective can mitigate poverty in an ecologically and socially sustainable manner (Lal and Israel 2006). MFIs and micro-enterprises can best foster sustainable development when they are "integrated in a view of community development that links the social, economic and environmental dimensions" (Vargas 2000). These build on the United Nations' call for sustainable development that includes these dimensions – economic objectives (growth, equity, and efficiency), social objectives (empowerment, participation, social mobility, social cohesion, cultural identity, and institutional development), and ecological objectives (ecosystem integrity, carrying capacity, biodiversity, and protection of global commons) (United Nations 1997, 171). In this growing acceptance that the earth is indeed shared (Brundtland Report 1987), there has been a growing trend to draw links between microfinance institutions and the need for ecological considerations in their businesses. We hope to explore those links in this thesis.

1.6 Strategic Sustainable Development

In conventional parlance, the terms "sustainability" and "unsustainability" are used within different contexts and are not always clearly defined. Within the microfinance context, it is perhaps easier to describe the concept of unsustainability by using the economic concepts of supply and demand. The demand on resources outweighs supply, and considering the current use of resources, scientists agree that there is a possibility that they might not meet the demand of future generations (Neumayer 2000, 307).

The world's population is increasing and totalled almost seven billion people as of 2011 (U.S. Census Bureau 2011). This growth brings with it a respective increase in the demand for resources such as food, fertile land, water, energy, and valuable resources. These resources are becoming increasingly scarce and their prices are increasing due to the laws of supply and demand (Costanza et al. 1997, 259). Social problems also abound as a result of greater reduction in access to clean water, air, and soil. There is also an increasing degradation of trust, which is often described as the social fabric that holds society together (Missimer et al. 2010).

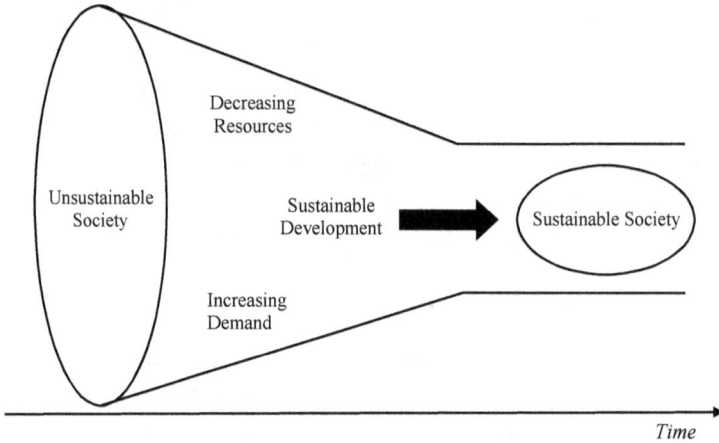

Figure 1.1. The funnel metaphor

Figure 1.1 is a visual depiction of the "funnel metaphor" representing the increase in demand for resources while there is a decrease in resources as time progresses. Society is moving in a direction with fewer and more costly solutions for its survival (Robèrt 2000, 244), thereby reducing the ability to manoeuvre. The challenge is to avoid hitting the walls of the funnel and find a way towards its opening, which represents a sustainable society (Robèrt 2000, 245). This situation, depicting society's unsustainable course and the problems it creates, can be considered the "sustainability challenge".

One instance is climate change, created by anthropogenic activities that have increased greenhouse gases and led to the melting of ice caps and increased sea levels and temperatures (Le Treut et al. 2007). These ocean temperature changes affect the currents of the oceans and disrupt weather patterns, creating more severe storms and even natural disasters such as floods, tornadoes, hurricanes, and landslides (Vellinga and Verseveld, 2000). This is only a miniscule sample of the wide array of environmental problems society faces today but can be used to illustrate the interconnectedness of the problems, as often the cause of one problem affects and creates many others.

Yet, there is a desire to continue growing, prosper, and – in the case of less affluent economies – escape poverty. One major factor to accomplish this is the access to the resources of the ecosystem, which at the same time have been manipulated and weakened by human activities. The magnitude of human impacts on society that has created the sustainability challenge is tremendous. The systematic aspects of these impacts are severe enough to threaten the ability of society to develop and ultimately survive. As illustrated in the funnel metaphor, if the walls of the funnel close in on society due to the systematic decrease in resources such as clean water, fertile lands, or clean air, an eventual collapse is probable. While cases such as the collapse of Easter Island (Diamond 1994, 363) provide a glimpse of the consequences of our actions, our understanding of the threshold or our ecosystem is indeed limited. For an MFI and its clients, the closing of the funnel walls could be seen as increasing regulations and potential fines, as well as increasing operational costs due to growing costs of electric power, water services, waste management, etc. For micro-borrowers, the decrease in affordable food and natural resources could be seen as hitting the funnel walls.

However, trying to address the numerous problems of the sustainability challenge is complex, since they are interdependent and in a pattern that is difficult to get an overview of (Robèrt 2000, 244). This leads to a situation in which it is difficult to know where to start in tackling the sustainability challenge. There is a clear need for a structured and comprehensive approach when trying to solve the sustainability challenge.

The idea of "development that meets the needs of the present without compromising the ability of future generations to meet their needs" (Brundtland Report 1987) provides the predominantly accepted definition of sustainable development. This description does not provide an answer to the question: What are the needs of the present? The complexity of the earth and its inhabitants make it challenging to draw a definition that encompasses all these areas. This is perhaps why society's unsustainable direction continues to create problems.

1.6.1 Backcasting from Sustainability

One way to meet these problems is through forecasting, i.e., predicting future challenges from current trends. For example, in order to reduce the incidence of pests, a farmer may use pesticides, which effectively manages the situation. However, this may poison the pollinating bees from a nearby bee farm (Gray 2009; Nyoni 2011). Given the consequences of the sustainability challenge and the fact that, with forecasting, planners are limited to "likely futures" and predictions based on past and current trends, a different method is needed.

This different method has been named "backcasting" (Dreborg 1996, 814) – a methodology where the planner begins by determining the desired state of success or goal and then asking: What do we need to do today to reach this goal? For our farmer, she could begin with a vision of a fruitful harvest – enough to make a profit and care for her family. She would then think through steps from that vision to her present circumstances. Here she could decide to use polyculture, crop rotation, or diversify to other forms of crops that are not susceptible to pests. She could even control insects by spraying with hot water, which has been shown to be as effective (Miller 2004). These alternatives will not only keep the bee farm thriving but also escape the harmful effects of pesticide. Forecasting identifies "likely futures" that can be predicted from present trends so that planners proceed with their view of what is realistic. Actions are often based on a continuation of present-day problem-solving methods projected into the future (Holmberg and Robèrt 2000). This amounts to a self-fulfilling prophesy, as planners become inherently limited by what they assume can be done. Consequently, forecasting builds on trends that are part of the problem. Backcasting, on the other hand, envisions future desired outcomes so that planners create actions from that vision to reach that goal (Holmberg and Robèrt 2000). Backcasting is therefore holistic. In this example, the pests could simply develop immunity to the pesticides used, which would require the farmer to use even more pesticides to the detriment of the crops. Backcasting, on the other hand, begins with a vision of the ideal farm, which incorporates farming, pest management, and operations, among others.

Backcasting has thus been likened to chess, where every move and step is directed towards the envisioned goal (Dreborg 1996, 814). Due to the complexities of the system, backcasting – rather than forecasting, which relies on current trends to predict likely outcomes of the future – is suitable for planning for sustainability. Backcasting can be done from scenarios of success, allowing for planners to describe their ideal scenario and create a simplified image of success. Building upon the imagery of the scenario has advantages such as being good for emotionally charged decisions and has been found to be useful for financial institutions to reduce taking on too much risk. However, it has its limitations, as it is more difficult for people to agree upon their ideal scenario due to differences in values, backgrounds, as well as changing technologies, among others. Planners are therefore encouraged to backcast from basic principles, i.e., conditions that must be met for a system to continue in a certain state. The complexities of the system where the planning takes place makes it impossible to predict all possible future outcomes. When backcasting from principles and from the vision of a sustainable society, planners constantly keep the goal in mind, and work towards it without being restricted by current trends. Backcasting from principles makes it easier to reach consensus, to deal with the uncertainties of the future, and to draw upon the full benefits of changing technologies. When done right, backcasting can increase the benefits of handling ecologically complex issues in a systematic and coordinated way and address today's societal challenges associated with current unsustainable actions (Holmberg and Robèrt 2000).

With sustainable development, the future is created by four conditions that need to be met in order to reach full sustainability. These conditions are the Sustainability Principles, reproduced below. They were created for the sustainable development process through an iterative and peer-reviewed consensus process by an interdisciplinary and international community (Robèrt 2002). They are a strategic response to the sustainability challenge and are a way to avoid downstream problems that could be created by traditional planning methods, as illustrated by the example of the farmer and the bees.

Since their initial publication, the Principles have undergone several revisions (Ny 2009, 6). They were designed to be based on a scientifically agreed upon view of the world; necessary to achieve sustainability; sufficient enough to achieve sustainability; general enough to structure all of society's activities relevant to sustainability; concrete enough to guide actions and serve as a "lighthouse" in problem solving and analysis; non-overlapping or mutually exclusive in order to facilitate comprehension and structured analysis of issues (Waldron et al. 2008).

The first three Principles describe direct and indirect anthropogenic deterioration of the biosphere regarding ecological sustainability, while the fourth emphasises the need for a strong social fabric in order to move towards social sustainability. The four Sustainability Principles (SPs) are worded:

"In a sustainable society, nature is not subject to systematically increasing:
concentrations of substances extracted from the Earth's crust;

- concentrations of substances produced by society;
- degradation by physical means;
In that society...
people are not subject to conditions that systematically undermine their capacity to meet their needs" (Ny et al. 2006).

1.6.2 Framework for Strategic Sustainable Development (FSSD)

As described above, the Sustainability Principles are robust and sufficient enough to *backcast* from in order to facilitate planning and make decisions within the complex sustainability challenge. The numerous problems creating the sustainability challenge that society is facing can be addressed "upstream" by avoiding creating problems at the root. Examples could be mining practises as well as logging. This is more efficient than addressing problems "downstream" or symptoms, exemplified by polluted sources of water and landslides due to clear-cutting.

While *backcasting* from the Sustainability Principles is effective for a visioning process, it is only one aspect of the efforts towards sustainability. The Framework for Strategic Sustainable Development (FSSD) – a systematic and strategic approach to sustainable development – effectively supplements the SPs as a decision-making tool. The FSSD was built as a simple, concrete, scientific-based framework for sustainability (Holmberg and Robèrt 2002, 294). It has been developed together with the international nongovernmental organisation The Natural Step (Robèrt 2002).

Due to the complexity of the wide array of interrelated problems described above, a framework for planning in complex systems is necessary. The FSSD allows for a "bird's-eye" view to better understand the sustainability challenge and the socio-economic system. Being able to use the same language in addressing the sustainability challenge is essential. The FSSD allows for the development of a common language to refer to the sustainability challenge and to create the purpose and the vision of success. It is a strategic and structured approach that helps planners manage complexity. Backcasting from the scientifically accepted Principles provides a robust platform to address the sustainability challenge society faces. It also provides prioritisation questions to serve as a defence mechanism to ensure planners stay on course towards sustainability. The FSSD is made up of five interrelated but distinct levels, as represented below:

SYSTEMS	Interactions between society and the ecosphere, including socio-ecological laws and norms.
SUCCESS	Society in compliance with socio-ecological sustainability: the Sustainability Principles.
STRATEGIC	Used to prioritise actions that have been backcast from success. Questions to ask: Is the action a step in the right direction? Does it offer a flexible platform, i.e., can it be developed upon? Will it give sufficient return on investment – cultural, financial, social, ecological, etc.?
ACTIONS	Concrete steps to move towards sustainability.
TOOLS	These may be systems or capacity tools that support decision-making. They may measure, build capacity, help implement actions, help better understand systems, and manage procedures, among other things.

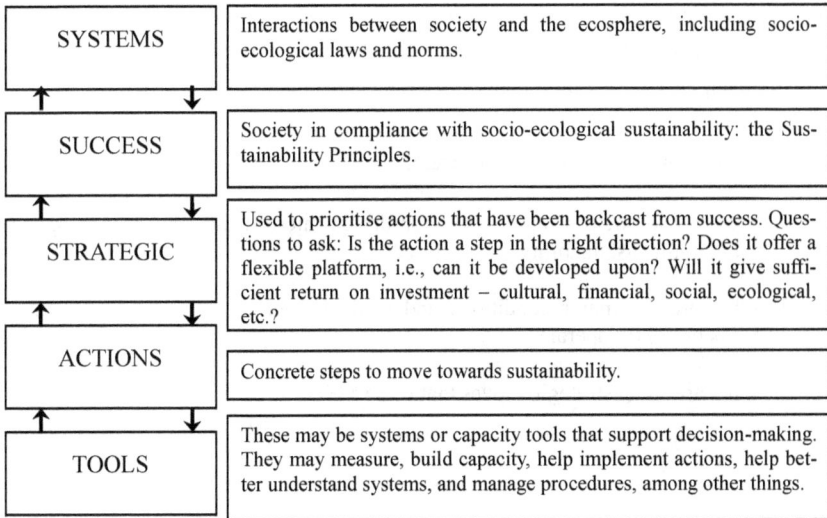

Figure 1.2. The Framework for Strategic Sustainable Development

1.7 Scope of Study and Research Questions

Our thesis seeks to explore why and how a full sustainability perspective can be of benefit to socio-economic mission-driven microfinance institutions. As stated earlier, poverty is much too complex to expect a single solution. It can, however, be tackled by a number of tools. Based on substantial evidence that microcredit is "an important financial tool for some households" (Banerjee, Duflo, Glennerster, and Kinnan 2010, 4) and raises the income and assets of some participants (Anderson, Locker, and Nugent 2002, 96), microcredit can be regarded as one of those tools.

We therefore chose to explore how a sustainability perspective can help microfinance institutions maximise their goals for the alleviation of poverty and well-being of their clients in a sustainable manner. "Sustainability" is defined to include socio-economic and ecological benefits, as elucidated by the Sustainability Principles.

Our research focussed on developing economies where the conventional opinion holds ecological sustainability as external to socio-economic growth. We hoped to extend the knowledge on application of full sustainability to relatively less affluent economies. Our intended audience are policymakers and executive management in the MFI sector and stakeholders. Our paper explores how taking a sustainability perspective in the core business of MFIs – rather than externalising it as a mere standard – would help them reach their goals in a sustainable manner.

Consequently, our research questions were:

1. How would socio-economic mission-driven microfinance institutions operate using a full sustainability perspective?

2. What are the major conditions under which socio-economic mission-driven MFIs presently operate?

3. What are some strategic moves that these MFIs can take in this regard?

2 Methods

2.1 Research Design

Our thesis focussed on exploring the benefits that a socio-economic mission-driven microfinance institution could derive from taking a full sustainability perspective. To this end, we wanted to understand how the FSSD and the Sustainability Principles could help these microfinance institutions so that they would achieve their goals in a sustainable manner. We also set out to develop relationships between ecological sustainability – which comprises of the first three Sustainability Principles – and operations of socio-economic mission-driven MFIs, which are loosely focussed on the fourth Sustainability Principle. This was geared at understanding the links between full sustainability and what these microfinance institutions, like many other businesses, identify as their priorities: maximising success and managing risks.

In order to do this, we thought it prudent to clearly understand their operational framework and what MFIs perceive as risks and major challenges. We also wanted to understand the manner in which they regarded the sustainability challenge and their work on ecological sustainability. We hoped that, based on our understanding of strategic sustainable development, our thesis would help MFIs appreciate the benefits of taking a full sustainability perspective in meeting their priorities as well as the available opportunities.

Our research was structured in three iterative phases: creation of the model, data gathering and analysis, and model testing. Flowing from the principle of backcasting, we commenced the research process from the envisioned future: creating a principle-based model of the socio-economic mission-driven microfinance institution operating in compliance with the Sustainability Principles. This was done through a brainstorming process based on knowledge gained from our literature review and sustainability. At this stage, we built the MFI's perception of its system and of its success, as well as strategic guidelines. The model was continuously refined throughout the thesis period as we gathered information from the other phases and by deductive reasoning. The refining process was done with caution to avoid creating a model from current trends (forecasting) rather than from a full sustainability perspective. Towards the end of the thesis period, we included a level of detail, which was to clarify principles for the testing of the model in the third phase. These details were influenced by principles on microfinance such as the Principles for Investors in Inclusive Finance (PIIF 2011), the Smart Campaign and the Client Protection Principles, and Consultative Group to Assist the Poor's Key Principles of Microfinance (CGAP 2004). The model also incorporated language as the triple bottom line principle, which was used by a large number of our sample MFIs to refer to strict adherence to the equal principles of economic, social, and ecological sustainability.

In gathering data, we had 16 interviews with professionals whom we identified as experts in their fields. These included authors, researchers, and management-level executives of microfinance institutions and of development agencies. Authors and researchers were chosen based on the articles published in peer-reviewed journals as related to our subject. The management-level executives of the MFIs were chosen from the Microfinance Information Exchange, a database for microfinance analysis (The Mix 2011), and Forbes' ranking of the top 50 microfinance institutions (Forbes 2011). We contacted development agencies based on the relevance of their work to our thesis. Of these interviews, 10 were done via email while four were done using the telephone and Skype. We conducted telephone and email interviews with one expert and conducted an interview in person. The telephone and Skype interviews were generally semi-structured and exploratory, as we sent the experts our sample questions before the sessions in order to steer the conversations. The interviews were recorded with the permission of the interviewees and transcribed.

Questions asked during the data-gathering phase were primarily aimed at formulating the current reality of the socio-economic mission-driven microfinance institutions in relation to the existing structure and work on ecological sustainability.

The questions were divided into two categories. The first was geared at practitioners who either worked within MFIs or in development agencies whose work related to microfinance. This set of questions slightly varied in respect of their particular work in the field regarding ecological considerations. For example, questions to our expert at the Netherlands Development Finance Company (FMO) included details about the environmental and social risk-management tools for MFIs developed by the organisation. The second category was researchers and authors who had explored the area of microfinance within ecologically sustainable limits. A list of our experts and a sample of questions asked have been annexed as Appendix A and B, respectively.

We also collected data from the Trends in Microfinance 2010–2015 (Triodos Facet 2011) as well as reports by independent agencies, including the Centre for Study of Financial Innovation (CSFI). The CSFI's 2011 Banana Skins Report was the result of a survey of 533 stakeholders from 86 countries and multinational institutions in the microfinance sector. The report provided information on perceptions of risk within the sector. Our data gathering also included document content analysis of the websites of 87 India-based MFIs, whose names were available on the MIX database. This was used to gather information on the articulation of ecological considerations.

The data collected helped form the "current reality" for MFIs and was then compared with the model for the gap analysis. As with the model building, this was largely iterative. This stage also helped identify strategic actions towards sustainability that MFIs could take in the short-term for the greatest impacts.

The third phase involved sending the model to the experts, who we had interviewed in the first phase, for feedback. Each expert was given a clear description of the main goals of the thesis, an explanation of the FSSD, along with the research questions to better understand the context. From there, they were asked to give comments and find possible shortcomings. Based on their feedback, we made adjustments and sharpened the model. A copy of the preliminary version of the model along with the cover letter is attached as Appendix C.

2.2 Sampling: Rationale and Process

The intended audience for our thesis are socio-economic mission-driven microfinance institutions and the development agencies that work with them. This guided our sampling process. In selecting the MFIs we worked with, the first screening process was by the MFI's commitment to socio-economic sustainability, as defined by its mission and description of success as articulated on its website. These MFIs were further screened by references to ecological sustainability, as articulated on their websites and case studies carried out by researchers.

We chose predominantly socio-economic mission-driven MFIs rather than those primarily focussed on financial inclusion (banking as a means of servicing a sector of the economy) for a number of reasons. First, certain concessions are often required to be made as a short-term investment for the long-term returns of ecological sustainability. We considered these MFIs that were committed to one aspect of sustainability as being relatively "ready" candidates for moving towards sustainability. Second, we realised the significance of an organisation's core ideology, a "consistent identity that transcends product or market life cycles, technological breakthroughs, management fads, and individual leaders" (Collins and Porras 1996, 66). We focused on MFIs whose "core ideologies" fit into our research and also considered other financial inclusion-based MFIs. This was to provide a balanced perspective, since all MFIs share the same marketplace.

In reality, the microfinance market is not clearly delineated, as socio-economic mission-driven MFIs face similar challenges and often compete for the same clients as others. Therefore, to minimise sampling bias and error in our data, we also interviewed two experts in the "financial inclusion" subsector.

2.3 Expected Results and Risks in Methodology

We anticipated that, in practice, few socio-economic mission-driven microfinance institutions would incorporate the ecological sustainability angle into their businesses. We also expected that data would reflect the perception of ecological sustainability as an external standard that amounted to placing an additional burden on poor people.

The major risks in our methodology were social desirability bias and the danger of a self-fulfilling prophecy. Ecological considerations are deemed socially desirable and there is a tendency for respondents to provide answers that help them appear socially desirable. We tried to guard against this by asking specific questions in relation to claims as well as triangulation of data, largely by conducting Internet searches to verify specific claims.

We also acknowledge that creating a preliminary model before data collection, as guided by the backcasting approach, may have influenced the questions asked as well as the responses provided. While we tried to be as objective as possible, there is a possibility that our expectations may have been influenced by theory-driven data collection.

3 Results

3.1 Microfinance within a Sustainable Framework: The Model

Flowing from the principle of backcasting, we created our vision of what the socio-economic mission-driven microfinance institution could look like after taking a full sustainability perspective. This vision was largely to help us better understand the challenges in the present circumstances. Borrowing language from vision-building (Collins and Porras 1996, 74), we created a "vivid description" of the MFI strategically operating in a sustainable future:

The MFI enhances socio-economic well-being in an ecologically sustainable manner. It continuously innovates, meeting the growing needs of its clients, who recognise that their prosperity is interconnected with that of the environment.

While this description may suffice as a boardroom pitch, the complexities of practical business operations make it insufficient for planning. We therefore built a model of what the MFI's operations and interactions would look like. Keeping in mind George Box's caution that "all models are wrong, but some are useful" (Box 1987, 424), we relied on the holistic planning framework of the FSSD for a more concrete approach to plan from the vision of success. Further, realising that innovation in itself is rarely for the future and more for the present (Drucker 2007, 209), we left out the last two levels of the FSSD (actions and tools). This would allow each MFI to create particular actions and tools within the technological and particular circumstance of the "future".

All the feedback received was helpful, although we viewed some as being inapplicable for the purpose of this thesis. For example, suggestions to modify the model to include details in order to make it more "practical" were not taken, as the model was created specifically as a principle-based tool. In addition, we realise that providing a deeper level of detail for a model of a sector (instead of a specific company) might include too many particular details that could be inapplicable in certain cases. We have, however, included details of the feedback received in Appendix F.

3.1.1 Systems Level: Model

This MFI clearly appreciates the complexities of its relationships with the interconnected parts of the socio-economic and ecological systems. It understands its reliance on and contributions of its short-term and long-term decisions and their potentially "disastrous" consequences (Costanza, Daly, and Bartholomew 1991, 2; Ritz 2011). It uses its knowledge of ecological economics to maximise the opportunities and avoid the risks occasioned by the endangered global support system. It recognises that the value of ecosystem services may not be reflected in the global price system (Costanza et al. 1997, 259).

The MFI realises that its welfare – as well as that of its clients – relies on natural capital and ecosystem services and that their prices would inevitably increase as they become more "scarce" and stressed (Costanza et al. 1997, 259). Consequently, it manages its operations to insulate itself from the shock of this price jump by accounting for the natural and human resources it depends on (Hawken, Lovins, and Lovins 1999). While it realises that a "very precise estimate" may be impractical, it builds on the growing body of economic accounting procedures for ecosystem goods and services (Costanza, Daly, and Bartholomew 1991, 9; Costanza et al. 1997; Ko 2007).

The MFI's long-term accomplishments show compelling benefits of full sustainability (van Alteren 2011b). It clearly meets its financial and non-financial goals so that its credit base and clients' long-term prosperity are secure. In addition to enjoying profitability and longevity from its forward-thinking approach, it also strives to influence other stakeholders within and outside itself. This is not as much an altruistic perspective as stemming from its appreciation of the interconnectivity of all stakeholders and the realisation that ownership of the earth and its resources are preserved or lost by all. The microfinance institution also strives towards nourishing relationships with its community and engendering the building of trust within the community.

The MFI's core purpose largely remains unchanged: to provide services to optimise its clients' well-being within ecologically sustainable limits. The clients are the microfinance institution's reason for doing business. An analogy may be drawn with the manufacturing sector – the clients are the MFI's products. The MFI realises that the development of those clients is critical to its own well-being and it must play an active role in ensuring that clients are given the right skills to ensure success

(Oyebode 2011b). It therefore continuously seeks to know its clients and offers products and services that optimally meet their needs (Losse 2011; Ritz 2011b; Villanueva 2011).

Regarding its internal operations, the MFI appreciates its connections with borrowers, investors, its competitors, regulating bodies, policymakers, and other stakeholders. This comprehensive perspective of social relationships informs its decision-making and its goals within ecologically sustainable limits. It also informs its personnel management style. It realises that its staff is the core of its operations and has a "balanced board of directors that can guide management according to specific market needs" (Sharif 2011). The microfinance institution therefore empowers its staff towards innovative learning and mastery of their own personal vision and maximises their alignment with that of the MFI's purpose.

The model socio-economic mission-driven MFI is a "learning organisation" that continuously expands its capacity towards its vision (Senge 1990, 14). Its competitiveness lies in its ability to learn faster, stemming from its appreciation of the interrelatedness of a socio-ecological system. The MFI uses its knowledge of society's need for a healthy social fabric, conservation laws, laws of thermodynamics, principles of biogeochemical cycles, feedback loops, among others, for continuous growth. A visual representation of the MFI within the socio-ecological system is described in Figure 3.1.

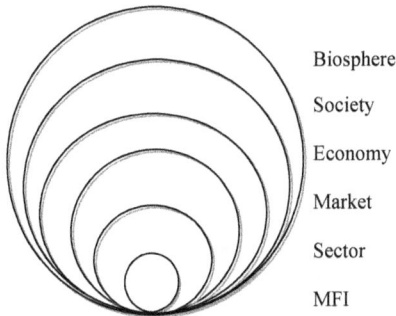

Biosphere

Society

Economy

Market

Sector

MFI

Figure 3.1. Model MFI within the socio-ecological system

The MFI further optimises its relationships with its local lending community to educate, influence, and create awareness in order to develop new ways to tackle and avoid social and ecological problems (Ritz 2011b). This empowers them for creating inventive local solutions (ibid).

3.1.2 Success Level: Model

The MFI defines success within the Sustainability Principles described in Chapter 2. While the visions of specific MFIs may be worded differently, they incorporate increasing the socio-economic well-being of clients in an ecologically beneficial manner. Success is also defined by the growth of its capacity and that of its staff to manage increasing complexities. Flowing from its appreciation of the systems level, it also measures success by the manner in which it continuously innovates in order to influence stakeholders in a manner that helps it meet its goals. These also lead towards longevity, which is important in provision of credit services (Ritz 2011b).

Success implies an MFI whose operations strive to eliminate contributions to systematic increases in concentrations of substances that are extracted from the earth's crust and produced by the society in addition to those that lead to the systematic physical degradation of nature. It also strives to eliminate its contribution to the undermining of people's capacities to meet their needs. It follows that an MFI that defines success as "the provision of financial services towards enhancing socio-economic well-being", for example, will automatically define "well-being" in terms of its elimination of contributions to the violations of the SPs and contributions towards a sustainable future. The MFI defines success within the Sustainability Principles described in Chapter 2 and as visualised below.

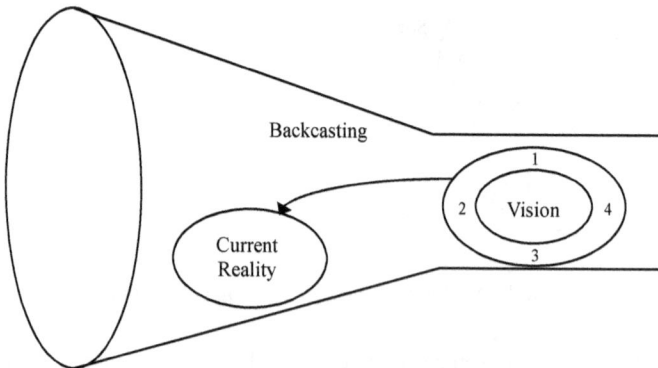

Figure 3.2. Vision within the Sustainability Principles

3.1.3 Strategic Level: Model

The strategic level of the FSSD outlines the principal planning methods that an organisation may use to *backcast* from its vision. At this step, it is important that the planning team creates explicit strategic guidelines to be able to prioritise the suggestions and derive the most promising actions at this level. After defining "success", the microfinance institution brainstorms for creative ways to bridge its vision with its present circumstances. This helps to keep the overall goal clearly in mind throughout the planning process. No decisions or judgements are made during the brainstorming process to ensure that participants are allowed to be as creative as possible when suggesting actions.

At its simplest, the MFI uses the three prioritisation questions discussed earlier, to screen these ideas. The first question – "Does this action proceed in the right direction?" – involves an analysis of the action against the vision of success (already defined within the SPs) and serves as a clarifying "sieve" in the metaphorical sense. For instance, a suggested action to provide access to cheaper genetically modified seeds would be screened as failing to enhance the client's long-term well-being (health wise) as well as the second SP, as it may flow from a systematic increase of substances produced by society. The second question – "Does this action provide a flexible platform for future improvements?" – nudges the screening process towards a long-term perspective. This question helps the MFI screen investments and actions that cannot be adapted or built upon in the long term. For instance, expanding in micro-franchising in a sustainable manner could be built upon as a means to expand its client base towards longevity of its business. The third question is: "Is this action likely to produce a sufficient return on investment to further catalyse the process?" This question builds upon the previous two using a pseudo balance sheet approach. A decision to use long-term funding sources for sustainable loans, for example, could be a move in the right direction as well as offer a flexible platform for future improvements. This decision could also result in financial returns on investment. Even better, long-term funding could translate into lower interest rates that would also produce political and social returns from its clients and the community in which it operates.

3.2 Current Reality

The assessment of the current reality was done through the lens of the Sustainability Principles informed by the Framework for Strategic Sustainable Development. We collected information on the activities of socio-economic mission-driven microfinance institutions. We also collected information on the primarily financial-inclusion-driven MFI subsector. As explained in Chapter 2, this was done to get what we hoped was a thorough appreciation of the current reality in view of the undifferentiated marketplace. MFIs, regardless of their purpose or operations, often compete for the same client base and are faced with the same challenges and opportunities. The information was then structured into the first three levels of the FSSD: the systems, success, and strategic levels. Then the information and characteristics of a current reality MFI was compared with that of the three levels of the model of the sustainable microfinance institution described in Chapter 3.1.

The current reality was written in principle-based language and details were provided for clarity. This was because, despite the shared challenges and opportunities, a generalised description would not do justice to the peculiarities of each market and the circumstances under which they operate.

Some information has been provided on the current reality in the introductory chapter. The data collected have been structured in the first three levels of the FSSD – systems, success, and strategic levels – as in Chapter 3.1 Due to the sensitive nature of the topic, some of the quotes in this section will be used without attribution. This is to respect the interviewee(s) need for anonymity.

3.3 Systems Level: Current Reality

At the systems level, socio-economic mission-driven microfinance institutions seem fairly aware of their interactions within society. Microcredit is largely perceived as a tool to reduce the poverty levels of the community in which they operate. Microfinance institutions are regarded as very important as they fill the gap that traditional banks cannot reach – financial services to the poor and other excluded communities (Drake 2011; Sharif 2011). A majority of the experts interviewed agreed that it was important that MFIs offered supplementary services such as business education and training. This aligns with the need to eliminate conditions that systematically undermine borrowers' capacities to meet their own needs. However, some respondents claimed that offering these additional services would merely overburden smaller and weaker MFIs. One expert explained that supplementary training was not an MFI's "core business". Another expert, however, opined that while these services should complement financing, in most cases, microfinance institutions are unable to afford additional considerations even if they know it is "good for them" to do so (Drake 2011). It was also opined that as "transaction cost and cost of intermediation [are some] of the biggest challenges faced by the microfinance sector ... MFIs [ought] to find strategic partnerships with business development and advisory services rather than taking on additional roles at this stage" (Sharif 2011).

We also explored the role of interest rates as a condition that systematically undermines the borrower's capacity to meet his or her needs. Microcredit is usually provided on a short-term basis at high interest rates (Asian Developmental Bank 2006, 1) due to the high operational costs of small-scale lending. Borrowers also tend to take multiple loans, which often go unguarded due to the absence of credit records. These loans and over-indebtedness trap borrowers in negative spirals so that they are unable to repay loans and meet their own needs (Barta and Bellman 2010). Over-indebtedness of clients has also led to the preponderance of credit risk for MFIs (Annibale 2011). A number of MFIs provide microcredit at relatively low rates for social needs such as education. For instance, Rang De educational loans are at 9 per cent (Ramakrishna 2011).

In many cases, microfinance institutions suffer from a funding mismatch, as they have to manage short-term funding for the medium or long-term loans that are optimal for their client base (Oyebode 2011). This is related to limited affordable capital, which trickles down to their inability to act as an effective tool to eliminate contributions that systematically undermine their clients' capacity to meet their own needs. As one interviewee put it, "We could easily do 10 times [as many] more loans if we had the funding" (Ramakrishna 2011). However, we found increasing access to specially designated funds from development agencies such as the International Finance Corporation, the World Bank Group, and the Canadian International Developmental Association (CIDA), all of whom have policies that reward socio-economic and environmental endeavours. For example, CIDA's policy is to integrate environmental considerations into its decision-making and activities, and to work with its partners and developing countries at improving their capacity to promote environmentally sustainable development (CIDA 1992).

Few MFIs find strong connections between their operations and ecological considerations (Pallen 2011). One researcher explained that there seemed to be "a natural reluctance to ecological planning" as it is seen to "hinder a free market" (ibid). While a growing number of MFIs acknowledge the sustainability challenge evidenced by problems such as climate change and its impact on the poor (Sattaiah 2011; Annibale 2011), ecological considerations are not generally perceived as being a pressing risk (Annibale 2011). In response to our suggestions that these MFIs weigh socio-economic and environmental sustainability requirements equally, one interviewee stated: "not at this stage. You need to understand the demand side first". This is perhaps due to what is viewed as minimal contributions to the violations of the Sustainability Principles, which was described to the respondents. It does not help that smaller MFIs and, in some cases the larger ones, are struggling with meeting socio-economic aspects of their business. One expert stated: "[The microfinance sector is] still far from triple bottom line thinking as the social perspective isn't covered yet" (Ramakrishna 2011).

Responses to the need to recognise "environmental standards" in MFI operations varied, depending on the size of the MFIs. The larger and more publicly known MFIs seemed more aware of what they described as "environmental sustainability" requirements, as they often make environmental reporting standards for funding purposes. Investors are increasingly demanding for ecological considerations in the operations of their recipients and are "driving focus on sustainability" (Drake 2011). This is a prime driver of change (Annibale 2011; Drake 2011; Ritz 2011). One simplified example is Kiva's Green Loans, launched in April 2011. While Kiva is not strictly a microfinance institution as described in this thesis – as it acts as a hub for lenders rather than lends itself – loans to "borrowers who want to make their businesses and communities more sustainable by reducing waste, recycling and minimising pollution" (Kiva 2011), exemplifies the growth in this area. The smaller MFIs were reluctant to regard environmental standards as part of their operations.

Responses typically viewed ecological considerations as burdensome and expensive, even though "the financial sector is increasingly asking for it" (Annibale 2011). One interviewee explained that it seemed inequitable for MFIs to incorporate ecological standards since it was not the case in the retail banking sector. As the expert put it: "You don't have links to client behaviour when giving a credit card." One researcher explained that the immediate perception is that socio-economic mission-driven MFIs need not incorporate additional "burden" by way of ecological considerations, as it amounts to market interference (Pallen 2011). Another interviewee explained that there was presently no way to "guarantee that the clients won't harm the environment" (Drake 2011). One proponent of environmental sustainability explained that unless these considerations "make economic sense... [they] will not fly" (Pallen 2011). Another expert explained that there has not been evidence of "causality between adopting [social and environmental] principles and being more successful [but that MFIs] do it because they want to [rather than] because they have to" (Drake 2011). It was suggested that incorporating these considerations in the loan criteria was one way to minimise costs, as it would occur as part of the due diligence process (Pallen 2011). However, the same interviewee stated that this may be limited to larger microloans and not for the smaller-sized ones (ibid). An expert from a development agency explained that the sector may not be "mature enough to focus on this niche area."

There is a lack of shared language on what constitutes "environmental" or "ecological" considerations on a "day to day basis" (Drake 2011). In addition, references to "sustainability" in the MFI sector often refer to financial independence.

Internally, MFIs appear to suffer from inadequate staff with the proper education and experience (CSFI 2011). The Banana Skins Report shows that MFIs are seen to be "institutionally weak in the areas of corporate governance, management quality and staffing" (Lascelles and Mendelson 2011, 7) and that staff capacity was a "recurring theme, with several respondents bemoaning the scarcity of good people with expertise in microfinance" (ibid 30). Staffing was deemed a "strong area of concern" and categorised as "operational risk: weakness in the back office, the management of technology, and the quality of staff" (Lascelles and Mendelson 2011, 11). Quoting an official of the Central Bank of the Philippines, regulated MFIs "must contend with increasing competition, and provide a wider scope and range of services while aiming for sustainability" (ibid).

This may be related to the insufficient financing. Mission-driven MFIs are often understaffed and spread thin, with staff working in multiple roles and under stress

(Pallen 2011; Ritz 2011). There is, however, a realisation that MFIs need to build "capacity to develop [innovative] products" (Annibale 2011). It does not help that the microfinance sector is highly competitive due to the insurgence of other non-traditional providers of credit services such as correspondent banking (Drake 2011; Lascelles and Mendelson 2011). This emphasises the need for management's capacity to make decisions as well as provide organisational learning.

On the major risks facing the microfinance sector, we found that credit risk constitutes the biggest widespread risk. In the Banana Skins Report for example, 75 per cent of respondent countries mentioned credit risk as one of their biggest risks (Lascelles and Mendelson 2011, 8). Another fast-rising risk is increased perception of negative reputation. For instance, "reputation" moved up to 2nd place of the biggest risks in 2011 from its 17th place in the 2010 rankings (Lascelles and Mendelson 2011, 7).

Some MFIs related health and safety considerations to credit risk, which is a high threat to MFIs. These concerns are often associated with the ecological sustainability of the local communities. The International Labour Organisation (ILO) estimates that two-thirds of workers in developing countries suffer from conditions that do not meet minimum safety standards with "heavy workloads, multiple tasks, and exposure to health risks such as poor hygiene, sanitation, and nutrition; parasitic disease infection; repetitive motion stress; and exposure to smoke, solvents, chemicals, heavy metals, fungicides, toxic gasses, corrosive acids; etc…" (Hall et al. 2008). One of the reasons for this lies in competitiveness and an effort to minimise costs from safety and health equipment and measures (Wenner, Wright, and Lal 2004). Paradoxically, an unhealthy work environment results in accidents or sickness of workers and could lead to sick days or periods away from work, which may affect their ability to pay back the loans (Oyebode 2011). Ecology, health, and safety are directly tied together, as society depends on natural resources every day such as clean air, water, and soil, which, if polluted, creates a direct health and safety impact on the borrowers and society as a whole.

3.3.1 Success Level: Current Reality

Some MFIs expressed their socio-economic mission in terms of benefits to ecology, with language such as to "raise clients' awareness about environmental impact" (Sattaiah 2011), "to organise groups of committed poor women and provide innovative financial services in a sustainable manner with a view to eradicate poverty through viable income generation activities" (Asirvad 2011).

Most of the experts from the MFIs we interviewed explained that their organisations were primarily focussed on a social sustainability premise, with missions ranging from the reduction or alleviation of poverty; "the enhanced participation of poor in economic development (Lawson 2011); "empowerment of 1 million families by 2013" (Aparna 2011); and helping "whole communities escape poverty and [ensuring] that the next generation is given good education" (Ramakrishna 2011).

In accordance with their socio-economic aims, many MFIs defined success as the well-being of their clients and the provision of complementary non-credit services, however limited. For example, one expert identified savings accounts as a way to help their clients build on their assets and increase their self-worth and pride (Mulwa 2011).

There seems to be a growing acceptance, albeit theoretically, of incorporating ecological considerations into socio-economic missions (van Elteren 2011; Mandal 2011). For example, of 87 India-based MFIs studied, 17 articulated ecological considerations, while fewer did so in practice. Some of the representatives of the MFIs interviewed, however, provided examples of attempts to meet both socio-economically and ecologically driven missions. For example, one MFI had trained 10,000 farmers in organic farming, methods of water reduction, and pest management practices (Sattaiah 2011). While these trainings or other activities are insufficient for a full sustainability perspective, they provide a glimpse as to the sector's behaviour towards it.

One interviewee suggested that ecological aspects of financing ought to be included in the interpretation of the social mission so that "social" will be interpreted to include ecological or environmental perspectives (Drake 2011). We did not find any MFI that took a full sustainability perspective in their operations.

3.3.2 Strategic Level: Current Reality

A large amount of work has been done on strategic guidelines for making decisions that incorporate environmental and social considerations into MFIs' operations. Most of these focus on the loan process, which is deemed to have the most leverage in the business (Drake 2011; Pallen 1997; FMO 2011). It also seems to imply that microfinance institutions that seek to incorporate ecological considerations must have incorporated these in their internal operations in the first place. The Netherlands Development Finance Company's (FMO) Environmental and Social Risk Management Tools appears to be the more developed and is used globally by hundreds of loan officers (FMO 2011). The FMO tools were created to incorporate social and environmental considerations into the operations of microfinance institutions. Its MFI Sustainability Guidance e-toolkit can be used by loan officers for detecting and preventing downstream health and environmental problems from microloans. Even though it is focussed on risk management, it also promotes best practices.

Viewing this tool from an FSSD perspective, it is a very useful and comprehensive mechanism to prevent and/or reduce negative environmental and social impacts. Its exclusion lists take a preventive stance that eliminates or reduces contributions to the violations of the Sustainability Principles. The tool can be used for strategic decision-making at the executive management level by offering a structure that helps prioritise possible actions. It further has a structure that allows the MFI to ensure a strategic perspective of the loan process by giving the loan officers a comprehensive tool that also includes follow up measures.

The Environmental Sourcebook for Microfinance Institutions, created by the Canadian International Development Agency, is another tool currently available for MFIs seeking to improve environmental management and the performance of their lending activities. It provides a background of the importance of a healthy environment to the success of micro-enterprises, and provides techniques for improving that environment. It also provides suggestions on how MFIs can turn environmental challenges into opportunities. The sourcebook focuses on sectors regarded as the most "notorious" in terms of adverse social and environmental impacts. These sectors include chemical-intensive agriculture and aquaculture, metalworking and electroplating, textiles and crafts, brick manufacturing, tanneries, small-scale mining, and foundries. On the challenges of reducing entrepreneurial activities that lead to adverse social and environmental consequences, without alternatives an expert opined: "that is the way the clients earn their livelihood" (Drake 2011).

Environmental and social indicators are also used in certain cases to assess client risk. As one expert stated: "...from our own practice, colleague development financial institutions [and] client banks... when you know the environmental and social performance of a client, you also have a better assessment of the client in terms of client risk, that is the risk whether a client will be able to repay its loan" (van Elteren 2011b).

Prioritisation processes for loans within the MFIs studied also varied. Some gave loans to a select group and for specific purposes, e.g. women for agriculture-related activities and business (Aparna 2011). After passing the first threshold, preferences were then given to loan applicants who passed specific rankings for accruable income, education levels, house ownership, and availability of peer guarantors, among others (Aparna 2011). Another prioritisation process used in the sector is the Smart Campaign's Client Protection Principles, which are socio-economic principles towards keeping clients as "the driving force of the industry" (The Smart Campaign 2011a). The principles include the avoidance of over-indebtedness, transparent and responsible pricing, appropriate collection practices, ethical staff behaviour, grievance mechanisms, and privacy of client data (The Smart Campaign 2011b).

Besides various guiding principles, discretion for choosing prioritisation strategies lie with the executive management. Almost all the interviewees expressed the significance of the role of an effective board and executive management in making decisions in the daily operations of microfinance institutions (Drake 2011; Lawson 2011; Mulwa 2011; Sharif 2011). Management information systems, while relatively expensive, were seen as important in facilitating the decision-making process by helping to manage loan portfolios and for tracking loans (Mulwa 2011; Ritz 2011). One expert pointed out an automated scoring model developed by Entrepreneurial Finance Lab had helped to reduce evaluation costs and default rates (Oyebode 2011).

Our research showed that the conventional assumption that incorporating ecological considerations was necessarily expensive was not accurate. Like any investment, ecological sustainability may introduce some costs in the short-term (Drake 2011). These costs may be financial, social, or cultural. A simple example is the introduction of energy-saving light bulbs. While they are pricier to buy initially, they pay back for the investment in savings in energy bills and the longevity of the bulbs. Other environmental saving methods, such as advocating re-use of materials, save money without any costs.

In any case, the problems that occur through unsustainable practices in the long run – such as erosion of soil, limiting the agricultural productivity of land, or contaminated bodies of water that require expensive solutions to recuperate them, along with the hidden or delayed costs that unsustainable practices represent – make a strong point that it might be better for business to take into account ecologically sustainable practices. It is in this regard that it has been suggested that the ecological perspective be incorporated into the social angle, so that the term "socio-economic" is defined as social and economic benefits within ecological considerations (Drake 2011; Triodos Facet 2011).

The microfinance institutions studied seemed to take decisions based on their socio-economic missions; actions are usually short term in nature and do not put much emphasis on their flexibility; return on investment is judged as financial and social (in relation to their clients). Table 3.1 highlights the differences between the model and current reality.

MODEL	CURRENT REALITY
Systems Level	Systems Level
Utilises ecological economics. Believes that its welfare as well as that of its clients depends on natural capital and ecosystem services.	Utilises traditional economic approach where the environment is deemed external to its operations.
Uses a systems-thinking approach towards its operations so that it views itself as interconnected to society within the biosphere.	Sees itself as independent from society and the biosphere. Economic, social, and ecological factors are deemed external.
Looks to create greater social contributions through empowering borrowers with services beyond financial dimensions. Promotes sustainable development (economic and social within ecological limits).	Looks to create economic and social contributions without emphasis as to whether it creates unintended consequences such as environmental degradation.
Success Level	*Success Level*
Defines its success within the constraints of not contributing to the violations of the Sustainability Principles.	Defines success as the socio-economic well-being of its clients.
Views success as upholding principles of honesty, transparency, accountability, human rights, etc.	Views success as upholding laws and regulations and economic requirements.
Strategic Level	*Strategic Level*
Uses the FSSD to facilitate planning and decision-making towards sustainability. Backcasts form its vision and prioritises from a full sustainability perspective.	Few MFIs currently use overarching decision-making frameworks. However, some use standards in managing their operations in an ecologically sustainable manner.
Maximises strategic tools and technologies that ensure its loan criteria and services are strategic towards sustainable development.	Few MFIs maximise available tools for loan criteria.

Table 3.1. Highlights of the model and current reality

4 Discussion

This chapter discusses the results in Chapter 3, our key findings, and attempts to test the validity of our findings and analyses. In doing this, we attempt to show why socio-economic mission-driven microfinance institutions ought to bridge the model representing full sustainability to the current reality. We also explore guiding criteria that microfinance institutions can use in order to maximise these benefits.

4.1 Analysis of Findings

Microfinance institutions do not generally regard ecological considerations as being a risk to their operations. At best, these concerns are deemed supplementary to the socio-economic mission. Even where references are made to "environmental sustainability", there are often differences between these claims and what the MFI actually does in that regard. The reason for this may lie in the absence of a shared language on what "environmental sustainability" means to a microfinance institution on a day-to-day basis. There is, however, a growing amount of work on making socio-economic-minded decisions in an ecologically sustainable manner. One of these is the environmental and social risk-management tools for MFIs developed by the Netherlands Development Finance Company (FMO) mentioned earlier. The FMO tools could be used to complement the Framework for Strategic Sustainable Development.

The chapter on results highlighted the differences between our perception of what ought to be ("the model") and what is ("the current reality"). Consequently, this section explores why socio-economic mission-driven microfinance institutions ought to take a full sustainability perspective.

4.1.1 Managing Credit Risk, Enhancing Reputation, and Minimising Competition

As stated in Chapter 3, credit risk constitutes one of the biggest risks faced by MFIs. While this risk has been linked to issues such as over-indebtedness, multiple lending, and weakness of internal controls, the fundamental reason for this is loan default. This is a fast-growing risk for an industry that, until recently, had "always prided itself on its '99 per cent' repayment record" (Lascelles and Mendelson 2011, 6).

We suggest that one way to stem incidences of loan default is by taking a full sustainability perspective that would incorporate a more comprehensive screening and due diligence process into the existing loan criteria. At its simplest, the loan criteria, which present an opportunity to maximise sustainability upstream, ought to minimise long-term social and environmental consequences of projects for which the loan is granted. Loans ought not to be granted to fund businesses that run on forced or harmful child labour as well as the purchase of synthetic and harmful pesticides or herbicides. In addition to an exclusion list, MFIs can maximise their socio-economic missions by incorporating ecologically sustainable alternatives that suit their various communities. For example, excluding agriculture based on harmful pesticides could help reduce risks of loan default caused by crop losses and assist their clients in maximising their access to loans by using cheaper substitutes to these chemicals. Harmful child labour also injures the community's socio-economic growth. A full sustainability perspective for the screening process could therefore help reduce incidences of loan default.

An MFI that emphasises health and safety requirements – as encompassed in the fourth Sustainability Principle, i.e., the elimination of contributions to conditions that systematically undermine people's capacity to meet their own needs – would also minimise its incidences of loan default and credit risk. An unhealthy work environment results in accidents or sickness of the entrepreneur or her workers, leading to sick days or periods away from work. This may affect the borrower's ability to pay back the loans. A full sustainability perspective would therefore help minimise credit risk by reducing incidences of loan default caused by accidents and adverse medical conditions.

The socio-economic mission-driven MFI operating from a full sustainability perspective would distinguish itself through its social impacts and profitability (Ritz 2011). It would develop its reputation as a contributor towards a sustainable society. This is perhaps even more important in view of the increased perception of a negative reputation being a major risk. A negative reputation may have a strong impact on business conditions and repels the main stakeholders: the borrowers and investors. Maintaining a good reputation will encourage and nourish the growth of the sector and individual microfinance institutions, as well as reduce unhelpful political interference.

A good reputation also has added advantages. An MFI can leverage its brand to increase its business, as it can reach clients and investors interested in ecologically responsible companies (Willard 2005, 135). It can also market to potential investors and employees who want to contribute to a meaningful cause. A full sustainability perspective can therefore translate enhanced reputation into improved competitiveness.

A good reputation could also lead to increased access to specially designated funds from development agencies such as the International Finance Corporation, the World Bank, and the Canadian International Developmental Association (CIDA), all of whom have policies that reward socio-economic and environmental endeavours. These types of policies would possibly expand as the need to differentiate between competing organisations grows. Additional access to subsidies and financing on favourable terms would not only help minimise the impacts of loan defaults but free up the MFIs funds to offer additional services such as business- or best-practice training, which have also been found to reduce loan defaults.

Portfolio expansion and the generation of additional revenues also help to improve the bottom line. In this case, the MFI can grow its revenues by exploring businesses in the sustainability arena. It may, for instance, explore energy dependency in developing countries. Grameen Shakti, a subsidiary of the Grameen Bank, is a suitable example. It provides loans for solar panels in Bangladesh, where 2006 figures showed that only 30 per cent of the country had access to the electric energy grid (Grameen Shakti 2011). Solar panels provide a substitute to diesel fuel power generators, which are dependent on fossil fuels that have increasing prices and contribute towards pollution (Islam, Islam and Rahman 2005, 678). These panels also often replace the use of kerosene lamps and the fumes they emit, which are harmful to human health. Additionally, the more independent and continuous electricity provided by solar panels allows for longer hours of production for micro-enterprises to increase earnings. Students can also benefit from longer hours of reading and studying time, allowing for further academic and personal development (Islam, Islam, and Rahman 2005, 678).

4.1.2 Improvement of Bottom Line

In addition to minimising credit risk, which increases fiscal efficiency, small-scale environmentally conscious practices in the internal operations of these MFIs can help improve earnings. Greater eco-efficiencies often lead to reduced waste of economic resources, including financial, material, and time resources. Thus, responsible use of resources such as water, energy, material, or waste is not only of ecological benefit, as less stress is placed on the ecosystem, but it is also economically sound (Pallen 1997; Wenner, Wright, and Lal 2004, 113).

Eco-efficiency is a management philosophy that focusses on achieving the "delivery of competitively priced goods and services that satisfy human needs and enhance the quality of life while progressively reducing ecological impacts and resource intensity throughout the life-cycle to a level at least in line with the earth's estimated carrying capacity" (World Business Council for Sustainable Development 2000, 9). While eco-efficiency is deemed particularly attractive for manufacturing-type businesses, using less water, energy, paper, and materials is something that can be done by any type of organisation and can be viewed as leading to lower operational costs and therefore increased profits. In the case of microfinance, the increased profits assist a borrower or MFI in becoming financially sustainable, and therefore more resilient. Costs saved from these eco-efficiencies could be steered towards other sustainability-based investments. For example, savings from reduction of water-use using a rainwater collection system could help finance the purchase of a solar panel.

It has been said that increased efficiency may not by itself translate into sustainability (Giampietro and Maumi 2008). This is due to the paradox that eco-efficient companies may become more competitive and increase their businesses, leading to the consumption of even more resources so that improvements in eco-efficiencies are overcompensated for by a rebound effect (Figge and Hahn 2004, 178). We, however, suggest that this can be managed using the holistic analysis process of the FSSD for its decision-making.

Basix India is one example of how eco-efficiencies or best practices can be beneficial to the MFI sector. The MFI taught farmers a systemic rice intensification method, which involved a 70 per cent reduction in the amount of water traditionally used in rice farming, leading to better use of water and higher yields of the paddy (Sattaiah 2011).

Furthermore, organisations that use the triple bottom line approach for measuring results and include the price of ecosystem services in their balance sheets, may find that social and environmental results outweigh financial benefits.

4.1.3 Organisational Learning

Microfinance institutions, like any organisation, are only as good as their employees and management. An organisation's ability to learn faster than the competition is the only sustainable competitive advantage (Senge 1990, 8). It is therefore important that the staff and management of microfinance institutions are given the opportunity to continuously expand their knowledge and skills. The fourth Sustainability Principle, which calls for the elimination of conditions that undermine people's capacity to meet their needs, embraces the need for understanding that can be satisfied by education. The MFI operating towards a full sustainability perspective therefore stands a better chance with a motivated and educated staff.

Cultivating a culture of learning could also help staff and management appreciate a full sustainability perspective in their work. This could build capacity for innovative product development towards meeting the MFI's goals.

A related concept to organisational learning is "systems thinking", i.e., "the ability to understand and address the whole, while examining the interrelationship between the parts" (Senge 1990, 54). The FSSD is built on a similar, albeit broader, concept, a systematic appreciation of the interrelationships between society and the ecosphere.

An MFI can apply the FSSD to create its own strategic plan for development.

4.2 Prioritising Actions

Microfinance institutions may need to take certain steps in order to enjoy the benefits that accrue from a full sustainability perspective. On the one hand, the physical consequences of social and economic needs may seem more urgent than seemingly external environmental concerns. On the other, we have shown that these concerns are far from "external" and are inherently connected to one another.

There are a number of existing tools and standards that aim to provide ways of measuring compliance with socio-economic and environmental sustainability. However, these standards, being of varied focus and details, may seem burdensome to smaller MFIs. We therefore sought to create what we hope are helpful guidelines, listed in Appendix D, for making operational decisions.

Yet, guidelines, as standards and tools, may conflict and appear ambiguous. We therefore suggest that decisions be made using a set of prioritisation questions. We have built upon the three questions under the strategic level of the FSSD. We hope MFIs find this useful in making decisions on a day-to-day basis.

4.2.1 'Right Direction'

This MFI could begin by asking: Is this investment or action in accordance with our vision? This could provide clarity on the decision to consider an action in the first place. We suggest that investments (financial or otherwise) be in line with the MFI's vision. This vision acts as a North Star, and every action navigates the MFI towards success.

Collins and Porras offer a thorough overview of how a company can articulate its vision in the article (Collins and Porras 1996). They explain that the vision is comprised of two main components: the core ideology (its core values and core purpose) and its envisioned future (10–30 year audacious goals and vivid descriptions of what it will be like to achieve the goals).

We also suggest the "Hedgehog" concept, a theory that aims at helping a company zero in on its strengths. Jim Collins suggests that a company ask three questions: What are we best in the world at (and what can we *not* be best at)? What drives our economic engine (in terms of profit – or in this case, ROI)? What are we deeply passionate about? (Collins 2001). The company then strives to find its vision where the answers to the questions intersect.

Where should we be?

What are we
passionate
about?

What can we
be the best in
the world at?

What drives
our economic
engine - what
provides the
most ROI?

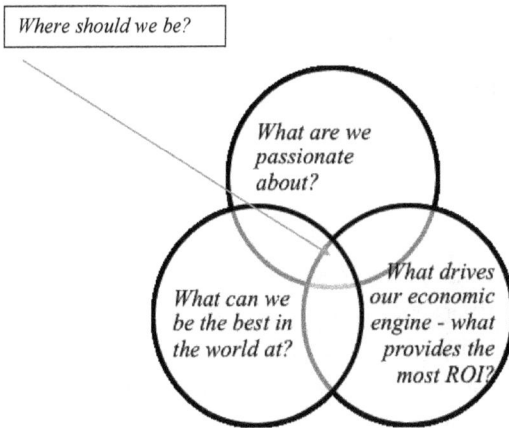

Figure 4.1. The "Hedgehog Concept"

As stated in 3.1.1, the vision is what the MFI seeks to achieve framed within the Sustainability Principles. It becomes even more significant in view of increasing recognition between the environmental and social performance of a client and client risk in terms of the client's ability to repay the loan, as explained in Chapter 3.

Using the vision as the first screening process may help the MFI avoid making decisions that are outside its interests. This should be balanced with a regular review of its vision, which will also keep it flexible.

4.2.2 Return on Investment

Microfinance institutions, like other organisations, thrive on some measure of effectiveness over the long term. It is perhaps more important when it comes to a banking business, since the client assumes that her savings are safe and that the bank will not go bankrupt and that she will be able to pay back the loan in small instalments.

One way to enhance longevity is financial resilience and a measurement of estimated financial returns from an investment. This measurement may, however, be insufficient by itself, as a company may derive even more benefit from social capital, the clients' well-being, ecological impacts, preservation of cultural values, visibility, employee satisfaction, and resource savings, among other things. As stated in the results chapter, incorporating non-financial aspects, such as ecological considerations, could help manage credit risk.

The estimated period for the return on investments and opportunity cost should also be considered so that higher ROIs score better than the others.

4.2.3 Flexibility

When a proposed investment passes the acceptable thresholds for compliance with the vision and estimated ROI, the MFI may then wish to consider its long-term flexibility. Actions on which other actions may be built upon should score higher than others. This helps create decisions in a strategic manner.

This rule helps to screen out investments that provide less than optimal benefits. The question to ask is: Does this action provide a flexibility platform for future improvements?

4.3 Validity and Limitations of Research

We attempted a rigorous study of our topic and triangulated our findings, taking care to minimise bias and aiming for the highest standards. However, we realise that certain limitations may arise due to our sampling. We acknowledge that the generalised findings on the current reality did not differentiate between geographical particularities, as this might have led to far-fetched conclusions. Further, many of the questions posed were of a sensitive nature. It is therefore likely that in some cases the interviewees gave biased answers and, despite our attempts, fell into the social desirability bias. This does not take away from our observations that the data collected was reliable.

5 Conclusion

Our conclusion provides a brief recap and a set of recommendations based on our research findings.

5.1 Recap

We began by defining poverty as a lack of opportunities for people to participate in society. Although microcredit is not the only tool or strategy to combat poverty, it has a direct and empowering approach that aid or relief does not always provide. The latter often makes recipients dependent. Traditionally, one problem has also been that the aid ends up in the wrong pockets.

The concept of microloans and microcredit for development has existed as a development tool for a long time. Its popularity and mainstream prominence was largely due to Dr Muhammad Yunus and the Grameen Bank being awarded the Nobel Prize in the year 2006.

The business of microcredit is often financially challenging. Small loans often equal high operational costs due to the amount of administration. Many socio-economic MFIs are also actively striving to keep interests low to provide decent loan conditions for borrowers. The result is often a dependence on external funding, which may be short-term, whereas the loans given might have a longer time span, which creates a credit mismatch.

The current situation within the microfinance sector is that the most progressive institutions focus on what is referred to as the double bottom line: financial and social inclusion. The ecological perspective is increasingly getting attention, even though many claim that poverty alleviation must be given priority and that adding a new perspective will only create an additional burden to the borrower.

At this point there is more and more evidence of society's unsustainable development. There is no one answer on how to move society in a sustainable direction. The advocates for full sustainability within microcredit argue that the sector should be included in this challenge. According to them, the rationale can be found on the micro- as well as the macro level. Unsustainable work conditions, such as use of harmful chemicals and pesticides, can poison waters and soils. In addition to causing health problems, it might also create a situation whereby repaying loans becomes increasingly difficult. Climate change is also said to hit poor people harder than the more affluent, forcing the poor to adapt to changed living conditions.

At an aggregated level, the microfinance sector makes a significant impact on the environment. An estimated 128 million people world-wide received microcredit in 2009 (Reed 2011). To include the sector in the combat against climate change and other environmental problems is at the same time a great challenge, largely due to a perception of placing an extra burden on the financially disadvantaged borrower. The solutions, or mitigations, that have been proposed provide ways to introduce the ecological perspective, including detecting harmful practices, in a cost-efficient and beneficial manner to all stakeholders. Furthermore, it has also been said that it is of great importance to present alternatives that raise awareness among the borrowers of the risks they are running and the possible solutions that might improve their situation.

Our thesis used a distinct approach to suggest strategic moves for embracing the full sustainability perspective, referred to as the Framework for Strategic Sustainable Development (FSSD). This has been developed as a framework for planning and decision-making, directly targeting the sustainability challenge. By taking this comprehensive and structured approach, we were able to see how MFIs could align their visions of success and goals with those of the Sustainability Principles, and from there backcast to the current reality with this end-goal in mind.

One of the most important findings was that the business rationale for taking on a full sustainability perspective must be clearly articulated. As one of the interviewees put it: "...otherwise it will never fly" (Pallen 2011). Awareness of environmental sustainability in the microfinance sector is generally low, even though there are some tools available designed to support management and loan officers in this regard.

Based on our research findings, we conclude that a full sustainability approach is beneficial to microfinance institutions. The strongest rationale is reduced credit risk, increased reputation, increased competitiveness, and improved earnings.

Although there are a number of challenges towards taking on full sustainability, doing so would actually help socio-economic mission-driven MFIs address many of the problems the sector faces, as well as bring with it a number of significant benefits.

In terms of being strategic and playing a greater role towards societal growth, if MFIs take on a sustainable development approach and adhere to the Sustainability Principles, not only will MFIs be providing a valuable service to the poor, but they will be providing a valuable service towards a more sustainable society.

Among the things we did not expect to find in our research that we did was that ecological considerations within microfinance were not something new. We found clusters focussed on trying to get the microfinance sector to embrace ecological considerations as well as health and safety practices.

Additionally, we found that the language and wording of the FSSD was found to be confusing to both the MFIs and experts we spoke to in the field.

5.2 Suggested Areas for Future Research

A key feature of the feedback received on the Sustainability Principles and the model was on the "technicality" and "theoretical" nature. First, we realise that the FSSD is principle-based to allow its users to amend it to their particular circumstances. Second, the model of a sector, as opposed to a particular company, ought to provide minimal details, which may not apply in the specific circumstances of each MFI. Yet, we realise the benefits of carrying out further research on using the FSSD for particular case studies and look forward to the findings that will arise from that. We also suggest additional research on utilising the FSSD for MFIs in developing economies, along with detailed monitoring of the economic impacts of embracing sustainable practices, which would improve upon the maximising of benefits from full sustainability for the sector.

5.3 Recommendations

Based on our findings, we conducted a brainstorming session in order to come up with a number of actions targeted towards socio-economic MFIs that wish to take a full sustainability perspective. These actions are divided into seven key areas. Within each of these areas, we conducted a prioritisation process guided by the questions referred to in 4.2 (right direction, flexible platform, and ROI) to determine what we suggest are particularly strategic initiatives that could be done within a relatively short period.

In addition to the list below, we have included a matrix highlighting the prioritisation process in Appendix E.

Establish the foundation. In order to act strategically, it is important that the organisation appreciates the sustainability challenge and the rationale for moving towards sustainability. We suggest that executive management engage stakeholders and agree on defining the vision, core values, and mission within the Sustainability Principles. This will provide the foundation on which further actions may be built upon. Our research found that there is an absence of a shared language on what "environmental sustainability" means to a microfinance institution on a day-to-day basis.

Utilise Eco-efficiencies. Based on our research findings, there is a genuine concern about keeping operational costs low for microfinance institutions due to the high costs associated with granting many small loans. This is particularly important for those aiming to keep service and interest rates low, while at the same time covering their costs and, when possible, making a profit. MFIs and their clients can benefit from eco-efficiencies through reductions in resources such as water, energy, fuel, and waste. These measures could provide economic, social, and environmental benefits, one of which is cost-savings. The increased competition in the market also has MFIs looking for any possible advantage, which would make them and their clients more resilient. It is anticipated that these savings may be invested in other sustainable development investments. For example, savings from reduction of water-use using a rainwater collection system could help finance the purchase of a solar panel.

Leverage on Loan Process. Our research suggests that the loan process offers a high leverage point for MFIs to maximise the socio-economic and ecological benefits. It is where MFIs can have the greatest control over the impacts of the activities of its clients (Drake 2011; Pallen 1997; FMO 2011). This increased control will help MFIs reduce loan default as a better assessment of the client in terms of client risk, offers insight as to whether the client will be able to repay its loan (van Elteren 2011b). This prevents unsafe and unhealthy work environments and allows MFIs to reduce their own risk of financing activities that are detrimental to society, such as micro-enterprises that support child labour or highly polluting activities.

There are existing strategic guidelines such as the FMO's Environmental and Social Risk Management Tools and its sustainability guidance e-toolkit, CIDA's Environmental Sourcebook for MFIs, as well as the Client Protection Principles. These can be used towards screening out less beneficial projects and enhance potentially sustainable ones.

Build Capacity for Staff. Our research findings indicated that a recurring theme for MFIs is that they often experience a deficiency in the capabilities of their staff, which is critical to them (CSFI 2011; Sharif 2011). Consistent training and capacity-building can help boost an organisation's development. We suggest that building the staff's capacity may not only lead to increased efficiency of the organisation's goals but will also help create a positive work atmosphere, leading to a higher retention of staff, which in turn reduces the cost of recruiting and training new employees.

Offer Complementary Products and Services. From literature and our interviews, we found that many MFIs and industry stakeholders believe MFIs need to offer additional services that will empower their borrowers, and represents an additional product and service to offer to expand their portfolio. Business training, health education, and training on beneficial agricultural practices can help to reduce incidences of loan default. These also amount to a measure of social responsibility and service to its clients, as they empower the borrowers and could improve the reputation of the organisation. We propose that enhanced reputation could help it secure partnerships that minimise the costs of these services.

Connect with Impact Investors. Our research found that one of the greatest concerns of MFIs is their funding. Socio-economic mission-driven MFIs that are forward-thinking and work with environmental initiatives can seek out impact investors, development banks, and funds that support these initiatives. For instance, impact investing is a fast-growing sector and environmental considerations are a growing trend in the greater consciousness of investors (Annibale 2011). Kiva's Green Loans previously mentioned are a clear example of this. MFIs that differentiate themselves with an increased social and environmental approach can attract financing on favourable terms better than their competitors. This would offer a competitive advantage, which was found to be a great concern for MFIs in searching for leverage in an increasingly competitive sector.

Emphasise External Communications. As mentioned before, many MFIs are experiencing increased competition. A means to meet this challenge is through the use of external communications. This can help create greater awareness about the operations of the MFI and also improve a reputation, which was shown in the research to be a major concern. In practise, this could mean publishing stories about its clients' successes in the socio-economic and environmental arenas. The MFI could also become active in the public debate through thought leadership. Building an image of being a front-runner could help it differentiate its brand, leading to increased competitiveness.

Reference List

Alkire, Sabina, and Maria Emma Santos. 2010. Acute multidimensional poverty: A new index for developing countries. *Oxford Poverty & Human Development Initiative (OPHI)*. Working Paper (July): 38. Available from: http://www.ophi.org.uk/wp-content/uploads/ophi-wp38.pdf (accessed 15 March 2011).

Anderson, C. Leigh, Laura Locker, and Rachel Nugent. 2002. Microcredit, social capital, and common pool resources. *World Development* 30(1): 95–105.

Annibale, Robert. 2011. Skype interview by authors. February 25.

Aparna, R.V. 2011. Email interviews by authors. April 9.

Armendáriz, Beatriz, and Jonathan Morduch. 2010. *The economics of microfinance.* 2d ed. Cambridge, Massachusetts: MIT Press.

Arora, Sangeeta and Meenu. 2010. Microfinance intervention – An insight into related literature with special reference to India. *American Journal of Social and Management Sciences* 1 (September): 44–54.

Asirvad Microfinance Private Ltd. 2011. Vision and mission. Available from: http://www.asirvadmicrofinance.co.in/ (accessed 3 May 2011).

Atkinson, A.B. 1987. On the measurement of poverty. *Econometrica* 55(4) (July): 749–764. Available from: http://www.jstor.org/stable/1911028 (accessed 14 February 2011).

Banerjee, Abhijit, Esther Duflo, Rachel Glennerster, and Cynthia Kinnan. 2009. The miracle of microfinance? Evidence from a randomized evaluation. Available from: http://econ-www.mit.edu/files/4162 (accessed 9 April 2011).

Barta, Patrick, and Eric Bellman. 2010. India journal: Microfinance by the numbers. *The Wall Street Journal,* November 15.

Bennett, Lynn, and Carlos E. Cuevas. 1996. Sustainable banking with the poor. *Journal of International Development* 8 (March-April): 145–52.

Booth, Charles. 1887. *Inhabitants.* London: British Library of Political and Economic Science (B.L.P.E.S.), Booth Collection. Quoted in Gillie, Alan. 1996. The origin of the poverty line. *The Economic History Review*, New Series 49(4) (November): 715–730. Available from: http://www.jstor.org/stable/2597970 (accessed 14 February 2011).

Box, George E. P., and Norman R. Draper. 1987. *Empirical model-building and response surfaces*. New York: John Wiley & Sons.

Broad, Robin. 1994. The poor and the environment: Friends or foes? *World Development* 22 (June): 811–822.

Brundtland Report. G. Brundtland (ed.) 1987. *Our common future: The world commission on environment and development*. Oxford: Oxford University Press.

CIDA (Canadian International Development Agency). 1992. *CIDA's Policy for Environmental Sustainability*. Available from: http://www.acdi-cida.gc.ca/inet/images.nsf/vLUImages/Policy2/$file/ENV-nophotos-E.pdf (accessed 5 April 2011).

Chen, Shaohua, and Martin Ravallion. 2007. Absolute poverty measures for the developing world, 1981-2004. *Proceedings of the National Academy of Sciences of the United States of America.* 104/43: 16757-62. Quoted in Chen, Shaohua, Martin Ravallion, and Prem Sangruala. 2009. Dollar a day revisited. *World Bank Economic Review* 23(2): 163–184 Available from: http://wber.oxfordjournals.org/content/23/2/163.full (accessed 15 February 2011).

Collins, Jim. 2001. Good to great: Why some companies make the leap... and others don't. New York: HarperBusiness.

CGAP (Consultative Group to Assist the Poor). 2004. *Key principles of microfinance*. Available from: http://www.cgap.org/gm/document1.9.2747/KeyPrincMicrofinance_CG_eng.pdf (accessed 8 April 2011).

Cornford, Robyn. 2002. Microfinancial services: What do Pacific people need? *Asia Pacific Viewpoint* 43 (December): 343–354.

Cosmopolitan. 1911. Quoted in *National Geographic*, 2 March 2011. Available from: http://momentscount.com/topics/authors/national-geographic/ (accessed 15 March 2011).

Costanza, Robert, Ralph d'Arge, Rudolf de Groot, Stephen Farberk, Monica Grasso, Bruce Hannon, Karin Limburg, Shahid Naeem, Robert V. O'Neill, Jose Paruelo, Robert G. Raskin, Paul Suttonkk, and Marjan van den Belt. 1997. The value of the world's ecosystem services and natural capital. *Nature* 387(15) (May): 253–260.

Costanza, Robert, H. E. Daly, and J. A. Bartholomew. 1991. Goals, agenda, and policy recommendations for ecological economics. In *Ecological economics: The science and management of sustainability*, ed. Robert Costanza, 1–20. Columbia University Press: New York.

Diamond, Jared. 1994. Ecological collapses of past civilizations. *American Philosophical Society* 138(3): 363–370.

Drake, Deborah. 2011. Skype interview by authors. April 8.

Drucker, Peter F. 2007. The classic Drucker collection: The essential Drucker. Oxford: Elsevier Ltd.

FMO. 2011. Social and environmental management guidance for micro finance institutions. Part B: Field guide. Available from: http://www.fmo.nl/FMO/documen ts/ESG/Part%20B-Field%20guide.pdf (accessed 10 February 2011).

Gillie, Alan. 1996. The origin of the poverty line. *The Economic History Review*, New Series 49 (November): 715–730. Available from: http://www.jstor.or g/stable/2597970 (accessed 14 February 2011).

Gowdy, John, and Jon D. Erickson. 2005. The approach of ecological economics. *Cambridge Journal of Economics* 29 (March): 207–222.

Grameen Shakti. 2011. Organic Fertilizer Program. Available from: http://www.gshakti.org/index.php?option=com_content&view=article&id=61 &Itemid=65 (accessed 23 March 2011).

Gray, Louise. 2009. Pesticides blamed for killing bees. *Daily Telegraph*. Available from: http://www.telegraph.co.uk/earth/wildlife/6157395/Pesticides-blamed-for-killing-bees.html (accessed 22 April 2011).

Greeley, M. 1996. Poverty and well-being: Problems for poverty reduction in role of credit. In *Who needs credit? Poverty and finance in Bangladesh,* ed. Geoffrey Wood and Iffath Sharif, 83–96. Dhaka: University Press.

Hall, Joan, Liam Collins, Elizabeth Israel, Mark D. Wenner. 2008. The missing bottom line: Microfinance and the environment. Commissioned by the SEEP Network Social Performance Working Group Social Performance MAP 2008. Available from: http://www.microfinancegateway.org/p/site/m/template.r c/1.9.34581/ (accessed 11 March 2011).

Hamilton, Lawrence C., Richard L. Haedrich, Cynthia M. Duncan. 2004. Above and below the water: Social/ecological transformation in northwest Newfoundland. *Population & Environment* 25(6): 195–215.

Haque, Muhammad Sayeedul, and Mashiro Yamao. 2008. Can microcredit alleviate rural poverty? A case study of Bangladesh. Proceedings of World Academy of Science, *Engineering and Technology* 36: 663–671. Quoted in Arora, Sangeeta and Meenu. 2010. Microfinance intervention – An insight into related literature with special reference to India. *American Journal of Social and Management Sciences* 1 (September): 44–54.

Hashemi, S.M. 1997. Those left behind: A note on targeting the hard-core poor. In *Who needs credit? Poverty and finance in Bangladesh,* ed. Geoffrey Wood and Iffath Sharif, 248–257. Dhaka: University Press.

Hawken, Paul, Amory Lovins, and Hunter Lovins. 1999. *Natural capitalism: Creating the next industrial revolution.* Boston: Little, Brown and Company.

Hillman, Arye L. 2002. Review of the elusive quest for growth: Economists' adventures and misadventures in the tropics, by William Easterly. In *European Journal of Political Economy* 18 (November): 783–795.

Hilson, Gavin, and Abigail Ackah-Baidoo. 2010. Can microcredit services alleviate hardship in African small-scale mining communities? *World Development* (December): 1–13. Doi:10.1016/j.worlddev.2010.10.004.

Holmberg, John, and Karl-Henrik Robèrt. 2000. Backcasting from non-overlapping sustainability principles – A framework for strategic planning. *International Journal of Sustainable Development and World Ecology* 7: 291–308.

IBRD / World Bank (International Bank for Reconstruction and Development / The World Bank). 2008a. *Word development indicators: Poverty data – A supplement to world development indicators 2008.* Available from: http://siteresources.worldbank.org/DATASTATISTICS/Resources/WDI08supplement1216.pdf (accessed 15 February 2011).

IBRD / World Bank (International Bank for Reconstruction and Development / The World Bank). 2008b. *Environmental sustainability: An evaluation of World Bank Group support.* Available from: http://siteresources.worldbank.org/EXTENVIRONMENT/Resources/environ_eval.pdf   (accessed   15   April 2011).

Ikeanyibe, O.M. 2010. Human resource management for sustainable microfinance institutions in Nigeria. *Global Journal of Social Sciences* 8(1): 119–133.

International Energy Agency. 2010. C02 emissions from fuel combustion – Highlights. Available from: http://www.iea.org/co2highlights/ (accessed 22 March 2011).

Islam, A.K.M, Sadrul Mazharul Islam, and Tazmilur Rahman. 2006. Effective renewable energy activities in Bangladesh. *Renewable Energy* 31(5): 677–688.

Kaushal, K. K., and J.C. Kala. 2005. Nurturing joint forest management through microfinance: A case from India. *Journal of Microfinance* 7 (Winter): 1–12.

Kent, Lawrence. 1991. The relationship between small enterprise and environmental degradation in the developing world with emphasis on Asia. Maryland: Office of Small, Micro and Informal Enterprises, Development Alternatives Incorporated USAID. Available from: http://pdf.usaid.gov/pdf_docs/PNABJ335.pdf (accessed 9 April 2011).

Khandker, S. 2001. Does micro-finance really benefit the poor? Evidence from Bangladesh. Paper presented at Asia and Pacific Forum on Poverty: Reforming Policies and Institutions for Poverty Reduction, held by the Asian Development Bank. Manila. Available from: http://www.adb.org/poverty/forum/pdf/Khandker.pdf (accessed 17 February 2011).

Kirchgeorg, Manfred, and Monika I. Winn. 2006. Sustainability marketing for the poorest of the poor. *Business Strategy and the Environment* 15(3): 171–184.

Ko, Jae-Young. 2007. The economic value of ecosystem services provided by the Galveston Bay/estuary system. Texas Commission on Environmental Quality Galveston Bay Estuary Program. Available from: http://files.harc.edu/Projects/Nature/GalvestonBayEconomicValue.pdf (accessed 9 April 2011).

Kono, Hisaki, and Kazushi Takahashi. 2009. Microfinance revolution: Its effects, innovations, and challenges. *The Developing Economies* 48(1) (March): 15–73.

Lal, Abhishek. 2010. An overview of microfinance and environmental management. Available from: http://www.greenmicrofinance.com/files/An%20Overview%20of%20Microfinance%20and%20Environmental%20Management.pdf (accessed 7 April 2011).

Lal, Abhishek, and Elizabeth Israel. 2006. An overview of microfinance and the environmental sustainability of smallholder agriculture. *International Journal of Agricultural Resources, Governance and Ecology* 5(4): 356–376.

Lascelles, David, and Sam Mendelson. 2011. *Microfinance banana skins 2011: The CSFI survey of microfinance risk – Losing its fairy dust.* United Kingdom: Centre for the Study of Financial Innovation.

Le Treut, H., R. Somerville, U. Cubasch, Y. Ding, C. Mauritzen, A. Mokssit, T. Peterson, and M. Prather. 2007. Historical overview of climate change. In *Climate change 2007: The physical science basis. Contribution of working group I to the fourth assessment report of the Intergovernmental Panel on Climate Change,* ed. S. Solomon, D. Qin, M. Manning, Z. Chen, M. Marquis,

K.B. Averyt, M. Tignor, and H.L. Miller, 93–127. Cambridge and New York: Cambridge University Press.

Losse, Karen. GTZ. 2011. Email interviews by authors. April 4.

MacFarquhar, Neil. 2010. Banks making big profits from tiny loans. *New York Times*, April 13. Available from: http://www.nytimes.com/2010/04/14/world/14microf inance.html (accessed 27 December 2010).

Mandal, Soumalya. 2011. Email interview by authors. April 5.

Maslow, Abraham. 1943. A theory of human motivation. *Psychological Review* 50(4): 370–396.

Matin, Imran, David Hulme, and Stuart Rutherford. 2002. Finance for the poor: From microcredit to microfinance services. *Journal of International Development* 14(2): 273–294.

Max-Neef, Manfred Antonio Elizalde, and Martin Hopenhayn. 1991. *Human scale development: Conception, application and further reflections.* New York: The Apex Press.

Missimer, M., K.H. Robert, G. Broman, and H. Sverdrup. 2010. Exploring the possibility of a systematic and generic approach to social sustainability. *Journal of Cleaner Production.* 18(10–11): 1107–1112.

Moll, Henk A. J. 2005. Microfinance and rural development: A long-term perspective. *Journal of Microfinance* 7(2) (Winter): 13–32.

Mulwa, Carol. 2011. Email interview by authors. March 23.

Nitin, Bhatt, and Shui-Yan Tang. 2001. Making microcredit work in the United States: Social, financial, and administrative dimensions. *Economic Development Quarterly* 15(3): 229–241.

Nobel Prize. 2010. *The official website of the Noble Prize.* Available from: http://nobelprize.org/nobel_prizes/peace/laureates/2006/ (accessed 27 December 2010).

Ny, Henrik, Jamie P. MacDonald, Göran Broman, Ryoichi Yamamoto, and Karl-Henrik Robèrt. 2006. Sustainability constraints as system boundaries: An approach to make life cycle management strategic. *Journal of Industrial Ecology* 10(1–2): 61–77.

Ny, Henrik. 2009. Strategic life-cycle modelling and simulation for sustainable product innovation. Ph.D. Diss., Blekinge Institute of Technology.

Nyoni, Stanley. 2011. Personal interview with author. Geneva, Switzerland. February 23.

Olivares-Polanco, Francisco. 2005. Commercializing microfinance and deepening outreach? Empirical evidence from Latin America. *Journal of Microfinance* 7(2) (Winter): 47–70.

Oyebode, Akintunde. 2011. Email interviews by authors. March 22.

Pallen, Dean. 1997. Environmental sourcebook for micro-finance institutions. Available from: http://www.encapafrica.org/meo_course/Course_Materials/Mo dule9--Special_Topics/MSMEs/Environmental_Sourcebook_for_Micro-fina nce_Institutions.pdf (accessed 9 April 2011).

Pallen, Dean. 2011. Skype interview by authors. February 25.

PIIF (Principles for Investors in Inclusive Finance). 2011. Available from: http://www.unpri.org/files/2011_01_piif_principles.pdf (accessed 27 March 2011).

Ramakrishna, N.K. 2011. Skype interview by authors. February 28.

Ravnborg, Helle Munk. 2003. Poverty and environmental degradation in the Nicaraguan hillsides. *World Development* 31(11): 1933–1946.

Reed, Larry R. 2011. State of the microcredit summit campaign report 2011. Available from: http://www.microcreditsummit.org/SOCR_2011_EN_web.pdf (accessed 23 April 2011).

Ritz, Anna. 2011. Interviewed by authors. Karlskrona, Sweden. February 9.

Robèrt, Karl-Henrik, Bio Schmidt-Bleek, Jacqueline Aloisi de Larderel, George Basile, J. L. Jansen, Ruediger Kuehr, Peter Price Thomas, M. Suzuki, Paul Hawken, and Mathis Wackernagel. 2002. Strategic sustainable development: Selection, design and synergies of applied tools. *Journal of Cleaner Production* 10(3):197–214.

Robert, Karl-Henrik. 2000. Tools and concepts for sustainable development: How do they relate to a general framework for sustainable development, and to each other? *Journal of Cleaner Production* 8(3): 243–254.

Robèrt, Karl-Henrik. 2002. *The Natural Step story: Seeding a quiet revolution.* Gabriola Island: New Society Publishers.

Roemer, Michael, and Mary Kay Gugerty. 1997. Does economic growth reduce poverty? Paper presented at the Consulting Assistance on Economic Reform

(CAER 11) Project. Harvard Institute for International Development/ USAID. Available from: http://pdf.usaid.gov/pdf_docs/Pnaca655.pdf (accessed 14 February 2011).

Sattaiah, D. 2011. BASIX India. Email interview by authors. April 5.

Schreiner, Mark. 2001. Seven aspects of loan size. *Journal of Microfinance* 3(2): 27–47.

Senge, Peter. 1990. *The fifth discipline*. New York: Doubleday.

Sharif, Harron. 2011. Email interview by authors. May 8.

Singh, Lokesh. 2011. Email interview by authors. April 4.

Sriram, M.S., and Samita Parhi. 2006. Financial status of rural poor: A study in Udaipur district. *Economic and Political Weekly* 41(51): 5269–5275. Quoted in Arora, Sangeeta and Meenu. 2010. Microfinance intervention – An insight into related literature with special reference to India. *American Journal of Social and Management Sciences* 1(1) (September): 44–54.

The Smart Campaign. 2011a. Campaign mission and goals. Available from: http://www.smartcampaign.org/about-the-campaign/campaign-mission-a-goals (accessed 9 April 2011).

The Smart Campaign. 2011b. The client protection principles. Available from: http://www.smartcampaign.org/about-the-campaign/smart-microfinance-and-the-client-protection-principles (accessed 9 April 2011).

Triodos Facet. 2011. Business principles. Available from: http://www.triodos.co.uk/en/about-triodos/who-we-are/mission-principles/business-principles/ (accessed 23 March 2011).

United Nations. 1998. Statement signed by the heads of all UN agencies 1998. Quoted in Peter Townsend, 2000, *Breadline europe: The measurement of poverty*. Bristol: The Policy Press.

United Nations. 2007. Microfinance in Africa: Combining the best practices of traditional and modern microfinance approaches towards poverty eradication. New York: United Nations.

United Nations General Assembly. 1998. Resolution adopted by the General Assembly: UN A/RES/53/197. Available from: http://www.un.org/depts/dhl/resguide/r53.htm (accessed 16 February 2011).

United Nations General Assembly. 2000. Twenty-fourth special session. Resolution adopted by the General Assembly. S-24/2. Further initiatives for social development. Available from: http://www2.ohchr.org/english/issues/globaliza tion/docs/A.RES.S.24.2.pdf (accessed 16 February 2011).

U.S. Census Bureau. 2011. International Programs Center. Available from: http://www.census.gov/ipc/www/popclockworld.html (accessed 23 April 2011).

Van Elteren, Anton. 2011. Email and Skype interviews by authors. March 23.

Vargas, Maria. 2000. Community development and micro-enterprises: Fostering sustainable development. *Sustainable Development* 8(1): 11–26.

Vellinga, P., and W.J. van Verseveld. 2000. Climate change and extreme weather events. Gland: World Wildlife Fund for Nature. Available from: http://www.panda.org/downloads/climatechange/xweather.pdf (accessed 9 April 2011).

Villanueva, Jessica. 2011. Email interviews. April 4.

Waldron, David, Karl Henrik Robèrt, Pong Leung, Michelle McKay, George Dyer, Richard Blume, Roya Khaleeli, and Tamara Connell. 2008. Guide to the framework for strategic sustainable development. Blekinge Institute of Technology. Available from: http://www.ingenjorerformiljon.se/wp-content/uploads/2010/12/080512-Guide-to-the-FSSD.pdf (accessed 23 April 2011).

World Business Council for Sustainable Development. 2000. Eco- efficiency: Creating more value with less impact. Available from: http://www.wbcsd.org/web/publications/eco_efficiency_creating_more_value.pdf (accessed 10th April 2011).

Wenner, Mark D., Norman Wright, and Abhishek Lal. 2004. Environmental protection and microenterprise development in the developing world: A model based on the Latin American experience. *Journal of Microfinance* 6(1): 95–122.

Willard, Bob. 2005. *The next sustainability wave: Building boardroom buy-in.* Gabriola Island: New Society Publishers.

World Bank. 1978. Employment and development of small enterprises, sector. Sector policy paper. Washington DC: World Bank.

World Bank. 2001. Making sustainable commitments an environment strategy for the World Bank. Available from: http://web.worldbank.org/WBSITE/EXTERNAL/TOPICS/ENVIRONMENT/0,,contentMDK:20123152~menuPK:281634~pagePK:148956~piPK:216618~theSitePK:244381,00.html (accessed 20 March 2011).

Wright, Graham A.N. 2000. *Microfinance systems: Designing quality financial services for the poor*. London: Zed Books Ltd.

Zaman, H. 1999. Assessing the poverty and vulnerability impact of micro-credit in Bangladesh: A case study of BRAC. Policy Research Working Paper No. 2145, Washington DC: The World Bank. Available from: http://www.microfinan cegateway.org/p/site/m/tecccccccczmplate.rc/1.9.24570/ (accessed 14 February 2011).

Appendix A

List of Experts

Name	Title	Organisation	Country
Mr Robert Annibale	Global Director of Microfinance	Citi Microfinance	United Kingdom
Ms R.V. Aparna	Head Process	Asirvad Microfinance Private Limited	India
Ms Deborah Drake	Vice President of Investment Policy and Analysis	Accion International	USA
Mrs Bunmi Lawson	Managing Director/ CEO	Accion Microfinance Bank Limited	Nigeria
Ms Karen Losse	Senior Advisor	Deutsche Gesellschaft für Technische Zusammenarbeit (GTZ) Gmbh	Germany
Mr Soumalya Mandal	Programme Manager, Micro Finance	Vivekananda Sevakendra -O-Sishu Uddyan (VSSU Microfinance)	India
Ms Carol Mulwa	Country Manager, Kenya	Oikocredit	Kenya
Mr Akintunde Oyebode	Head SME Banking, Personal and Business Banking	Stanbic IBTC Bank Plc.	Nigeria
Mr Dean Pallen	Principal	Dean Pallen International	Canada
Mr N.K. Ramakrishna	Co-founder and CEO	Rang De	India
Ms Anna Ritz	Former employee	Tujijenge Microfinance (TMF)	Tanzania
Mr D. Sattaiah	Chief Operating Officer	BASIX	India
Mr Haroon Sharif	Head (Economic Growth Group)	Department for International Development (DFID)	Pakistan
Mr Lokesh Singh	Managing Partner	Sanchetna Financial Services	India
Mr Anton van Elteren	Senior Environmental Specialist	The Netherlands Development Finance Company (FMO)	The Netherlands
Ms Jessica Villanueva	MFI Program Coordinator	Inter-American Development Bank	USA

Appendix B1

Questions Sent to Researchers in the Microfinance Sector and Development Agencies

Background

Our thesis hopes to bridge current operations of microlending organisations (and microfinance institutions)[1] with a sustainable future. In a sustainable world, socioeconomic growth will be within an ecologically beneficial framework. Therefore, the best actions would not systemically[2]:

- ...lead to increase of substances from the earth's crust e.g. the use of fossil CO_2 and destructive mining.
- ...lead to concentrations of substances produced by society e.g. the use of harmful chemicals and pesticides, water pollution.
- ...physically degrade the earth e.g. overfishing, deforestation, erosion from excessive land use.
- ...undermine people's capacity to meet their needs, leading to lower trust and weakened social fabric e.g. child labour, exploitative working conditions.

We chose MLOs for their potential as a development tool and its inclusiveness. Our research is in three stages:

1. We want to better understand the central decision-making frameworks of MLOs.
2. Then, we will explore how MLOs can operate from a strategically sustainable perspective and the benefits that would accrue to them.
3. We will also highlight and explore how to bridge the gaps between (1) and (2), by understanding the barriers and the steps they can take to overcome them.

---

[1] At the initial phase of the research, the term 'MLO' was used. However, interviewees insisted that any differences were theoretical and interchangeable with 'MFI'.

[2] We describe 'systematically' as increased deviation from the natural state due to societal influence and increasing dependence on activities that cause these effects.

Your responses will help us validate the information received from MLOs and in building a framework for sustainable MLOs.

Questions

Our research has shown various perspectives on the rationale for and the actual benefits that accrue from microcredit. Some hold that these organisations ought to primarily act as poverty-reduction tools, while other opinions suggest that it is sufficient that they provide financial services to a section of the economy (low income, poor people). In your view, which critical roles should microlending organisations play in society? What do you consider as the role of traditional MFIs (as delineated from other organisations e.g. credit unions, community banks etc.)? We would be most obliged if you could share your reasons with us.

Some microlending organisations as MFIs and impact investors, offer additional services including environmental and business education. Some research in this area shows that this may be effective in maximising the loan and increase payback rates. Others argue that it merely leads to increased transaction costs, which undermines the effectiveness of the loans. Would you please share your thoughts on this?

Microcredit is thought to be a potential development tool for its inclusiveness and community-based approach. We however recognised a number of challenges which they often face. In your view, what are the main challenges and why? Are these challenges intrinsically linked to the each MLO's organisational model?

Flowing from question (3), can you please share your views on optimal ways to meet these challenges?

Based on your experiences, which aspect of an organisation's decision-making framework is most significant in determining or undermining the success of these organisations?

A growing group of MLOs and MFIs focus on both social and environmental sustainability issues. Do you think that both the institutions and borrowers benefit from this perspective? Can you please share your opinion on this?

1. In your view, should MFIs equally weigh environmental sustainability standards with socio-economic standards? Do you think trade-offs play a significant role in this regard? We would be most obliged if you shared your thoughts on this.

Some research suggest that there are hardly any universal 'best practices' to address the needs of micro borrowers, who are in practice a diverse group with different needs. We propose that MFIs moving towards sustainability can benefit from an overarching framework. This would be a set of guidelines rather than specific actions. What are your thoughts on this? Would you propose any guidelines for sustainable microlending organisations?

Appendix B2

Questions Sent to Executives of Microfinance Institutions

The aim of this interview is to learn more about the main areas of relevance for microlending organisations (and MFIs)[3] in order help ensure their social, financial and ecological sustainability.

Questions

Mission, success factors and challenges

How would you describe the mission of your organisation?

How would you define success for your organisation?

What do you consider to be the biggest challenge(s) or barrier(s) for your organisation to reach success (as discussed above)? Could you share some thoughts on this?

What are the main measures/practices in your decision making process to ensure success, and how do you measure them/using specific metrics?

Loan making process

What do you consider to be the most significant considerations for granting loans? Do you use standard criteria or do they vary depending on the applicant and the purpose of the loan?

---

[3] At the initial phase of the research, the term 'MLO' was used. However, interviewees insisted that any differences were theoretical and interchangeable with 'MFI'.

External Factors

What is your opinion on government regulation of microlending organisations? What are the significant effects of regulation on your organisation?

Besides the clients, whom do you consider your most significant stakeholders? How much influence do they have on your operations and decision-making?

Recently the political interventions in the Indian state of Andhra Pradesh have generated substantial attention. Do you see this is an isolated case, or as a growing trend?

Ecological Sustainability

We observed that your organisation works with environmental sustainability. Can you please tell us more about this and the reason why your organisation choose to do so?

Within what areas of the organisation is it used? (In the loan criteria/clauses in loan contracts, education/training, promoting alternative solutions, etc.)

What have been the results so far? (Example: x amount of loans taken with ecological criteria, x amount of people trained, etc.)

1. Does this effort represent any extra costs for your organisation, if so, how are they distributed (are any of these costs subsidised)?

Does your organisation consider climate change to be a risk to your operations and your borrowers?

Would you be willing to let us cite your organisation as an MLO with good practises in our thesis?

Appendix C

Testing the Model: Preliminary Version and Accompanying Cover Letter

Dear [...]

We are most obliged that you have accepted to act as an expert to test our model of the strategically sustainable microfinance institution.

We have attached the model together with an introduction and an explanation of the most essential concepts used together with the theoretical framework our research and Masters' programme is built upon (the FSSD). We suggest that you provide comments on the following:

Comprehensiveness: From your standpoint are there any essential parts being left out or missing that should be there?

Clarity: Is there anything that is difficult to understand or unclear?

Accuracy: From an overall perspective, how do you view the model?

Suggestions: What do you think could be among the most strategic steps for an MFI to take, moving in the direction of the model?

You could leave your comments either directly in the document as tracked changes and comments, or in a separate email. We would be most grateful if we could receive your response by 3rd May 2011, which will give us sufficient time to include it before our submission on 9th May 2011.

We will be happy to make any clarifications any details if required.

Thank you.

Alejandro Turbay, Daniel Nordlund and Funmilayo Akinosi

Background, Methodology and Key Concepts

Stemming from a shared desire to learn more about the mechanisms behind micro-finance and poverty alleviation from the sustainability perspective, we chose to write our thesis on microfinance institutions that carry out their socioeconomic driven missions in an ecologically sustainable manner.

Goal

The aim of our thesis has been to examine how a full sustainability perspective (economic, social and environmental) can help mission-driven MFIs achieve their goals. In order to do so we developed a model of the ideal MFI operating in a sustainable manner (defined later in this text).

Methods

To establish a foundation from where the model could be developed, we interviewed a number of experts and practitioners within the microfinance sector and undertook an extensive literature review together with analysis of different industry publications and reports.

Theory

In order to better understand the model, below is an explanation of the main theoretical components which it is built upon:

FSSD (Framework for Strategic Sustainable Development). This framework is used by many organisations internationally for planning and decision making in complex situations. It is composed of five distinct but interrelated levels (Systems, Success, Strategic, Actions and Tools). For the purpose of the model, only the first three levels were used.

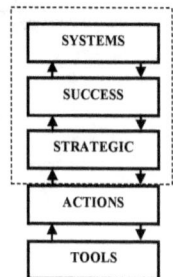

The Four Sustainability Principles (4SPs). This is a way to define sustainability based on firm scientific principles. They state that in the sustainable society, nature is *not* subject to systematically increasing:

i. Concentrations of substances extracted from the Earth's crust
ii. Concentrations of substances produced by society
iii. Degradation by physical means

and, in that society - iv. People are not subject to conditions that systematically undermine their capacity to meet their needs.

Backcasting. Finally, a planning methodology known as *backcasting* was used. Here planners begin by determining the desired state of success or goal and then ask: 'What do we need to do today to reach this goal?' In the case of the FSSD, the *backcasting* was done from complying with the Sustainability Principles.

The Model

Systems Level. Understanding the system in which the MFI operates, and the interactions that occur between society and the ecosphere, including socio-ecological laws and norms.

This MFI clearly appreciates the complexities of its relationships with the interconnected parts of the socioeconomic and ecological systems. It understands its reliance on and contributions of its short-term decisions and their potentially 'disastrous' long term consequences.

It uses its knowledge of ecological economics to maximise the opportunities and avoid the risks occasioned by the endangered global support system. It recognises that the value of ecosystem services may not be reflected in the global price system.

The MFI realises that its welfare, as well as that of its clients rely on natural capital and ecosystem services and that their prices would inevitably increase as they become more 'scarce' and stressed. Consequently, it manages its operations to insulate itself from the shock of this price jump by accounting for the natural and human resources it depends on.

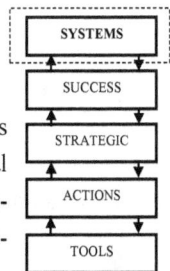

In addition to enjoying profitability and longevity from its forward-thinking approach, it also strives to influence other stakeholders within and outside itself. This is not as much as altruistic perspective as stemming from its appreciation of the interconnectivity of all stakeholders and the realisation that ownership of the earth and its resources are preserved or lost by all. The microfinance institution also strives towards nourishing relationships with its community and engendering the building of trust within the community.

The MFI's core purpose largely remains unchanged: to provide services to optimise its clients' wellbeing within ecologically sustainable limits. It therefore continuously seeks to know its clients so as to offer products and services that optimally meet their needs.

In respect of its internal operations, the MFI appreciates its connections with the borrowers, the investors, its competitors, regulating bodies, policymakers and other stakeholders. This comprehensive perspective of social relationships informs its decision making and its goals within ecologically sustainable limits. It also informs its personnel management style. It realises that its staff is the core of its operations. It therefore empowers its staff towards innovative learning and mastery of their own personal vision and maximises their alignment with that of the MFI's purpose.

The model socioeconomically driven MFI is a 'learning organisation' that continuously expands its capacity towards its vision. Its competitiveness lies in its ability to learn faster and stems from its appreciation of the interrelatedness of social and ecological factors. It uses concepts as society's need for a healthy social fabric, principles of biogeochemical cycles, feedback loops, among others for continuous growth.

Success Level. An MFI's defined state of success, within the constraint of not contributing to the violations of the Sustainability Principles.

The MFI defines its success within the constraints of not contributing to the violations of the Sustainability Principles (SPs) as described above.

While the visions of different MFIs may be worded differently, they incorporate increasing socioeconomic wellbeing of clients in an ecologically sustainable and beneficial manner.

Success is further defined by the growth of its capacity and that of its

SYSTEMS

SUCCESS

STRATEGIC

ACTIONS

TOOLS

staff to manage increasing complexities.

Flowing from its appreciation of the systems level, another way to measure success would be the manner in which it continuously innovates in order to influence stakeholders so that this helps it meet its goals. These also lead towards longevity, which is important in provision of credit services.

It follows that an MFI that defines success as 'the provision of financial services towards enhancing socioeconomic wellbeing', for example, will automatically define 'wellbeing' in terms of its elimination of contributions to the SPs and contributing to progress towards sustainability.

Strategic Level. How the MFI reaches its state of success. Which are the methods and strategies used to get there?

The Strategic level of the FSSD outlines the principal planning methods that an organisation may *backcast* from its vision. After defining 'success', the microfinance institution brainstorms for creative ways to bridge its vision with its present circumstances. No decisions or judgements are made during the brainstorming process as participants within the creation of goals are allowed to be as creative as possible. These suggestions are then prioritised at the strategic level. At its simplest, the MFI uses three prioritisations questions.

The first question: 'Does this action proceed in the right direction?' involves an analysis of the action against the vision of success (already defined within the SPs).

The second question: 'Does this action provide a flexible platform for future improvements?' nudges the screening process towards a long-term perspective.

The third question is: 'Is this action likely to produce a sufficient return on investment to further catalyse the process?'

Appendix D

Suggested Strategic Guidelines for Operations

Flowing from our literature review and expert interviews, we compiled a list of guidelines which a socioeconomic mission driven microfinance institution may use when taking a full sustainability perspective in its operations. These guidelines are far from exhaustive and derive their validity when used in compliance with the Sustainability Principles. They provide a glimpse of maximising the creative actions towards success. MFIs may also find some of these suggestions useful.

Equity. Operations must respect human rights, accountability and transparency, as well as be hinged on continuous improvement and respect for the environment towards the promotion of sustainable development.

Community Based. Actions ought to look towards collective improvements of society by enhancing the living conditions of communities rather than solely on the individual.

Co-learning. Our research has found that actions that are achieved through co-learning and co-creation are more resilient as learners and creators buy in to the vision.

Funding. MFIs should maximise long-term rather than medium-term funding sources. Long-term funding sources would suit its borrowers' long-term repayment needs.

Grievance Mechanisms. Transparent and responsive mechanisms for redress of grievances will help build trust and could provide political and social return on investment.

Continuous Innovation. MFIs should strive towards continuous innovation of financial products that suit their clients' needs. This ought to be balanced by the need to take reasonable steps to avoid over-indebtedness by extending credit to borrowers who demonstrate adequate ability to repay the loans.

Self-sufficiency. MFIs should look towards financial self-sufficiency as it underlines their independence and longevity towards their clients' benefit.

Managing Clients. MFIs should develop a structured approach to managing their clients, which may enhance the benefits of the loans. This could be done by regular visits by loan officers and reporting standards.

Complementary Services. Exploration of a wide range of products beyond financing that includes business training, health, best practices training, business and insurance loans as well as program to enable borrowers' children education may be helpful. This may be done in connection with specialised organisations, like NGOs in different fields.

Personal Development Plans for Employees. Clear professional development plans improve capacity and add to the work conditions that retain employees at MFIs.

Suggested Strategic Plan for Loan Criteria

While some of the suggested guidelines for the microfinance institution's operations will also apply to the loan criteria, our research identified specific actions which can be used for MFIs who want to maximise a full sustainability perspective in their loan criteria.

Incentivise Positive Behaviour. The loan processes should incentivise behaviour that complements socioeconomic aims in an ecological sustainable manner (as defined by the SPs). Here, proposed entrepreneurs who submit business proposals that do not comply with the MFI's socio-economic and environmental objectives are given alternative solutions rather than a general denial.

Positive discrimination for Certain Categories. Loan criteria should be poised at helping clients and their communities alleviate poverty and develop themselves. Consequently, loan terms for education or entrepreneurial projects, for example, should be on less stringent terms than other categories.

Enhance Trust Building. Loan criteria should enhance trust especially in group lending processes.

Knowledge sharing. The MFI is always focused on sharing its knowledge and experiences with the relevant stakeholders. This is done through publishing articles, case studies and participating in leading conferences.

Suggested Strategic Tools

There are already a variety of tools used by MFIs to build their capacity, act as indicators, evaluate, analyse, measure and assess their actions and strategy for success. Some have been highlighted below.

FMO's environmental and social risk management tools and the MFIs Sustainability Guidance e-toolkit. These enable a structured loan process where harmful operations can be screened as well as potential ecologically sustainable operations can be given sufficient support. Feedback and monitoring tools will also equip loan officers with appropriate technology to report pay back and loan defaults.

Entrepreneurial Finance Lab Tools, utilise a proprietary psychometric testing process of the entrepreneur's psychological profile, business acumen and honesty to measure risk and future potential. It has already been used in a range of developing economies and simulated impacts on samples show a 20-45% reduction in default.

Social and ecological reporting through a structured programme will help keep track of progress of meeting goals to alleviate poverty, maximise new business ideas in terms of ecological sustainability.

Sustainability reporting, where all major social and ecological achievements are presented will differentiate it from its competitors and place it in an attractive position for investors.

Audit and Performance tools will allow for tracking progress by annual environmental audits. One of such tools being presently used is the ISO 14001, and the entire ISO family of standards.

Appendix E

Brainstormed Activities

This outlines the prioritisation process for recommended actions.

Actions were assessed based on the ranking below. For each area, the highest ranking action is highlighted in green. When two actions got the same score the one judged being more strategic was chosen and marked with a (+).

Interpretation of Matrix

Area - Actions have been grouped to sectors and marked 'area'

- Specific action - Actions that come from the brainstorming session

Prioritisation question 1- Does it move in the right direction that is towards the organisation's vision within a full sustainability perspective?

Prioritisation question 2: Can the action be improved upon in the long-term?

Prioritisation question 3: Will it provide sufficient return on investment (whether financial, social, ecological, cultural etc.)?

- The prioritisation questions are Ranked 1 – 3, where 3 is the highest

Area	Q1	Q2	Q3	Total	Comments
	1 - 3	1 - 3	1 - 3		
1. Company culture					
1.	Build an in-depth understanding within the organisation of the sustainability challenge and the rationale for moving towards sustainability. Align goals, vision, mission and values with sustainability.	3	3	3	9+	A prerequisite to make the whole organisation move in the right direction.
2.	Create a shared language around sustainability.	3	3	1	7	To make everyone talk the same language and understand its meaning has a great importance.
3.	Create feedback loops to enhance the learning from past projects/individual clients' cases.	3	3	2	8	Key part of the MFI being a learning organisation.
4.	Identify sustainability 'champions' at all levels of the organisation. They should be specifically committed and ready to push all activities forward.	3	3	1	7	Voluntary basis. Should be given extra training and be ready to spread the knowledge.
5.	Establish the business case/rationale for moving towards full sustainability and create understanding and belief throughout the organisation that this will be the future within this sector - making it a possibility to be a front runner.	3	3	3	9	Key to make the organisation give its best. It is as important as understanding the FSSD since it is a management tool.
6.	Ensure that operations respect human rights, accountability and transparency, as well as be hinged on continuous improvement and respect for the environment towards the promotion of sustainable development.	3	2	3	8	A strategic guideline that should be implemented in the everyday work of the MFI.
2. Internal operations					
7.	Utilise eco-efficiencies in internal operations to benefit economically from responsible use of resources such as water, energy and waste. Also a good example for borrowers.	3	2	2	7	Sets a clear example of the ambitions of the organisation; internally and externally, it also supports the learning organisation concept.
8.	Investigate options for use of renewable energy.	2	2	2	6	Closely linked to the activity above.

9.	Ensure that management information systems incorporate sustainability efforts.	2	2	2	6	To ensure efficiency and structure.
10.	Utilise audit and performance tools, such as ISO 14 000, that will allow tracking progress by annual environmental audits.	2	2	2	6	Practical tools that support the organisations moving towards sustainability
3. Loan Process						
11.	Integrate existent loan process tools and criteria such as FMO's tools, the Environmental Sourcebook for Micro-Finance Institutions and The Smart Campaign as platforms to develop sustainability criteria.	3	2	3	8+	These are the most developed tools available that ensure needed structure and that the ecological perspective is included in a cost effective way.
12.	Provide possible alternatives to harmful operations (pesticides, chemicals, use of kerosene lamps and indoor stoves) having a negative impact on the borrowers, their communities, society and surrounding environments (contamination of air, erosion of productive soil, poisoning of drinking water etc.)	3	2	2	7	An important guideline and activity that makes the tools above even more operational.
13.	Ensure the loan officers have the right loan criteria to make the loan process efficient by understanding needs of borrowers, screening possible harmful activities and provide support to socially and ecologically beneficial alternatives.	3	2	2	7	The loan criteria ought to minimise long-term social and environmental consequences of projects for which the loan is granted.
14.	Establish systems for virtual/SMS/remote follow ups with borrowers in order to improve efficiency and keep costs low.	2	2	2	6	Prerequisite is that there is a mobile phone infrastructure.
15	Institute grievance mechanisms. Transparent and responsive mechanisms for redress of grievances will help build trust and could provide political and social return on investment.	2	2	2	6	To be trustworthy this guideline is of utmost importance.
16.	Establish relationships with specialised NGOs with expertise in different fields such as agriculture, energy and business to ensure best possible products.	2	2	2	6	Within certain areas it is not possible to provide all knowledge needed within the organisation.

No.	Recommendation					Rationale
17.	Utilise the Entrepreneurial Finance Lab (EFL) Tools. This utilises a proprietary psychometric testing process of the 'entrepreneur's psychological profile, business acumen and honesty to measure risk and future potential.'	3	2	2	7	A concrete tool that supports tools mentioned above. It provides unique information regarding the entrepreneurial profile of borrowers.
18.	Make constant product and process innovation part of the MFIs culture; incentivise ideas leading to new, innovative products (like an extra day off rather than bonuses due to constrained financial resources).	2	3	2	7	Innovation is a key to the long-term success moving towards the vision.
19.	Create a product development team for sustainability oriented loan products.	2	2	2	6	A designated team will give needed focus.
20.	Establish mechanisms to help over-indebted borrower out of negative spirals.	2	2	3	7	Important for collection purposes as well as social support system for borrowers.
21.	Ensure that loan criteria are poised at helping clients and their communities alleviate poverty and develop themselves. Consequently, long term loans for education or entrepreneurial projects, for example, should be on less stringent terms than other categories.	3	2	3	8	Puts forward the community perspective as well as education as two major components to the long-term success of alleviating poverty.

4. Staff

No.	Recommendation					Rationale
22.	Ensure that new employees are aligned with mission, vision and values of the organisation.	2	2	2	6	Commitment is a key factor for success.
23.	Make training and capacity building a priority of the organisation and create incentives. Prioritised areas should be environmental impact from different clients' operations and possible alternatives, business and health care.	3	3	3	9	Training is one part of the goal of constant innovation and being a learning organisation.
24.	Providing adequate working conditions for staff in terms of safety, health and workload.	3	2	2	7	Must be the foundation.
25.	Ensure that staff is qualified and is competent and receives a fair salary to retain them.	2	2	1	5	Skilled staff and high retention rates are key to success.
26.	Create environment with feedback mechanisms, systems for knowledge sharing and designated meetings for sharing experience and joint brainstorming.	3	2	2	7	One part of being a learning organisation.

5. Services						
27.	Constantly screen under-served borrowers/ segments/ communities.	2	2	3	7	MFIs tend to target the 'wealthier poor.'
28.	Provide adequate training/education within areas such as business, health, agriculture.	3	3	3	9	Have many positive effects such as reduced loan default and empowered borrowers.
29.	Establish procedures to work with whole villages/ neighbourhoods/communities to create societal changes. Capacity building can ensure leverage (this can go hand in hand with product development).	3	2	3	8	Closely linked to the loan criteria that targets whole villages.
6. Investors						
30.	Establish a reporting system that encapsulates sustainability efforts taken and how they have had a favourable impact on the conditions of the borrowers.	3	2	3	8	A major component to create needed trust with the investors and show long term commitment.
31.	Keep a constant dialogue with investors to report progress but also ensure that their demands and ideas are met as well as taken into account.	2	3	2	7	Closely linked to the action above.
32.	Clearly articulate the rationale behind full sustainability and plan to develop this further into the operations of the MFI (include understanding of sustainability challenges etc.)	2	2	2	6	This is something that should come in initial contacts with a new investor.
33.	Actively seek impact investors that share the goals and the mission of the organisation.	3	3	3	9	Creates strong bond and long-term commitment.
34.	Create and publish a sustainability report where all major social and ecological achievements are presented. This should be done at least every year.	2	2	2	6	Make efforts visible and strengthens the reputation making the MFI more attractive.
7. External communications						
35.	Develop show-cases that can be used to promote the benefits of sustainability thinking within the MFI-sector (should be about successful cases by the organisation).	2	2	2	6	Important tool in external communications. Success cases always speak loudly.
36.	Be active in the public debate. Present efforts and success stories and case studies. Communicate why sustainable development is favourable to borrowers.	2	3	2	7+	Makes the success cases public. Enhances the reputation of the MFI as a front runner.

37.	Develop a strategy for external communications (focusing on sustainable development) to align the messages used with the external world (media, investors, regulating bodies etc.).	3	2	2	7	Important to get structure and efficiency in communication and make it accessible internally.
38.	Ensure spokespersons have proper message/media training to successfully convey the main messages around sustainable development projects of the MFI.	2	2	2	6	Provide training if required to enhance quality of the communications.

Appendix F

Feedback on Model

The final version of the model of the sustainable microfinance institution, as presented in the thesis, was based on our initial version together with the suggested changes/improvements we received. Besides these comments we also received feedback that could not be applicable on the development of the model per se. They are presented below. The names of the interviewees have been withheld.

Theoretical Nature of Model

- *'My only comment is that it is very theoretical, but I guess it is supposed to be that way'* (Interviewee A).

- *'This seems to me a very theoretical, conceptual, almost hypothetical approach. If you really want to help MFIs there should also be a practical viewpoint, in terms of the business case and also ways how to reach that (using a toolkit, describing a step-by-step approach to implement sustainable practices, from awareness raising + defining policies, doing a pilot, into full implementation)'* (Interviewee B).

- *'The theoretical component is built on the use of The Four Sustainability Principles (4SP). What informed the selection of this method? In practice, MFIs could be easily evaluated using the Triple Bottom Line (TBL) which is a more practical approach. The concepts are similar so it might not be too much of an issue'* (Interviewee C).

Language

- *'Language wise, this is very difficult to understand. Sentences are not coherent and do not read well, especially IV [Sustainability Principle Four]. Suggest if this can be put in a positive way'* (Interview person B).

- *'You outline what nature is not aiming to do. Might it be better to formulate this in a positive way, so what nature is supposed to do?'* (Interviewee D).

UNIVERSITY MEETS MICROFINANCE

edited by PlaNet Finance Deutschland e.V.

ISSN 2190-2291

Abonnement

Hiermit abonniere ich die Reihe **University Meets Microfinance (ISSN 2190-2291)**, herausgegeben von PlaNet Finance Deutschland e.V.,

❑ ab Band # 1
❑ ab Band # ___
    ❑ Außerdem bestelle ich folgende der bereits erschienenen Bände:
        #___, ___, ___, ___, ___, ___, ___, ___, ___, ___, ___

❑ ab der nächsten Neuerscheinung
    ❑ Außerdem bestelle ich folgende der bereits erschienenen Bände:
        #___, ___, ___, ___, ___, ___, ___, ___, ___, ___, ___

❑ 1 Ausgabe pro Band   ODER   ❑ ___ Ausgaben pro Band

Bitte senden Sie meine Bücher zur versandkostenfreien Lieferung innerhalb Deutschlands an folgende Anschrift:

Vorname, Name: _____

Straße, Hausnr.: _____

PLZ, Ort: _____

Tel. (für Rückfragen): _____ *Datum, Unterschrift:* _____

Zahlungsart

❑ *ich möchte per Rechnung zahlen*

❑ *ich möchte per Lastschrift zahlen*

bei Zahlung per Lastschrift bitte ausfüllen:

Kontoinhaber: _____

Kreditinstitut: _____

Kontonummer: _____ Bankleitzahl: _____

Hiermit ermächtige ich jederzeit widerruflich den *ibidem*-Verlag, die fälligen Zahlungen für mein Abonnement der Reihe **University Meets Microfinance** von meinem oben genannten Konto per Lastschrift abzubuchen.

Datum, Unterschrift: _____

ibidem-Verlag

Melchiorstr. 15

D-70439 Stuttgart

info@ibidem-verlag.de

www.ibidem-verlag.de
www.ibidem.eu
www.edition-noema.de
www.autorenbetreuung.de

www.ingramcontent.com/pod-product-compliance
Lightning Source LLC
Chambersburg PA
CBHW070409200326
41518CB00011B/2125